MILES McKENNA

OUT!

HOW TO BE YOUR AUTHENTIC SELF

AMULET BOOKS • NEW YORK

Cataloging-in-Publication Data has been applied for and may be obtained
from the Library of Congress.

ISBN 978-1-4197-3994-1

Book design by Celina Carvalho and Tree Abraham

Printed and bound in China
10 9 8 7 6 5 4 3 2

Amulet Books are available at special discounts when purchased in quantity for premiums
and promotions as well as fundraising or educational use. Special editions can also be created
to specification. For details, contact specialsales@abramsbooks.com or the address below.

ABRAMS The Art of Books
195 Broadway, New York, NY 10007
abramsbooks.com

To every toy on misfit island.

To second-grade Miles. When you get older, Mom is going to buy you boxer briefs for Christmas and you get to cut your hair.

To you, as a reminder that you're never truly alone in this world.

CONTENTS

PART THREE:

PART FOUR:

FOREWORD

Dear Reader,

Being true to yourself and standing proudly in your identity is a gift not only to yourself but to everyone you meet. Shining as who you are—because who you are is something to be celebrated—helps everyone you encounter feel free to do the same. Queer kids often hear about how it gets better; and while that may give them the strength to keep going, it leaves them with a daunting question to figure out on their own: How do I get through all of this *now*? In a world that often makes queer kids feel like outcasts, coming out can feel impossible, and loving all of your identity can seem like an act of political resistance. I'm grateful that you get to navigate that world with Miles McKenna at your side.

For me, being gay felt like a secret I'd never be able to tell. I don't remember having many out and proud celebrities to look up to, gay musicians who sang about what I was going through, or even any queer friends or family whom I could ask advice or learn from. When I was figuring it all out, I couldn't go on the Internet and search "coming-out stories." But today, one search on YouTube will yield thousands of firsthand accounts, from almost every perspective under the queer umbrella. You can find bisexual boys talking about the stigma they face within the community, transgender women of color speaking out about the unique challenges they encounter in their everyday life, asexuals explaining how they realized their identity was valid, and gay couples sharing their adoption stories. The Internet has given a platform to so many queer people to finally tell their story in their own way—and has connected young queer people not only to their communities, but also to their history. One person I am honored to see lead the charge is Miles.

I first met Miles at—of course—a Pride event. Before I finally went up to introduce myself, I watched as he met a few of his adoring fans. Miles is one of the brightest young creators on YouTube, one I've been watching—completely in awe—for a while. He's got that X factor that every great creator has: a unique point of view, a fresh execution of creativity, a charm and a wit that draws you in, and a message that keeps you thinking. All of that in one person? It's a no-brainer that someone like that would find success in making YouTube videos.

But what set Miles apart for me was watching him connect with his viewers in person. He listened to them pouring their hearts out, some even breaking down in tears as they described how he helped them, or entertained them, or was there for them when they needed it most. He held their hands and looked them in the eyes with a sincerity that came from understanding exactly what they were going through—because he'd been through it too. He not only listened, but he also heard. And he truly made them feel seen, understood, and validated. He did it over, and over, and over, because the line to meet him was endless. Giving that much of yourself can feel heavy, but Miles did it with grace and humility. In watching Miles exude this grace, I turned from a fan into a superfan.

When Miles and I finally *did* meet after he was done meeting all the young kids who looked up to him, one of the first things he told me was that I had helped make his own coming-out journey easier, and that he wanted to do the same for kids like him—others who are questioning their identities and wondering how to gather the courage to tell the people they love. I reassured him that he was already doing exactly that, and he was the perfect person to carry out that mission.

Miles is a beacon of hope for so many young queer people, and I'm grateful for the amazing stuff he makes on the Internet. His videos have garnered millions of views around the world, and just by sharing his truth, he is literally changing the world. Not every creator takes this kind of opportunity seriously or understands the impact that they can have. While it's nobody's obligation to create videos for social good, I believe it's a missed opportunity when you don't use your platform to help those who look up to you. Watching Miles evolve over the years into one of the best creators on YouTube makes me feel like the future is in good hands, and that the queer kids today have someone who is on their side and ready to help. When I first found out Miles was going a step further and writing this book, I couldn't wait to read it and share it with anyone and everyone. A guide like this will save lives—plain and simple.

This guide doesn't read like a typical self-help book. Instead it's like taking a peek at Miles's personal journals, complete with brilliant anecdotes related to life-affirming questions (like choosing a name that best fits your gender expression) mixed with an incredible "gaylist" (a gay playlist . . . duh!) with bops to play at a cute little queer social event. This book is for so many kinds of people: teens who are questioning, parents hoping to understand, teachers wanting to learn so they can then teach. It works as a great personal companion as well as a guide for those seeking to be better support systems for their queer loved ones. Miles approaches his story with sensitivity and depth, but stays true to the very thing that made his fans—maybe you!—fall for him in the first place: his perfect balance of brutal honesty and hilarious introspection.

Miles does an incredible job acknowledging the weight of coming out while exploring what the experience really should be: a celebration. You're finally letting the people in your life know you better—what an incredible gift! And Miles has created a book that honors that celebration and shows how it all can actually be so much fun. Whether he's talking about experimenting with self-expression through new hairstyles or giving advice on delivering witty coming-out lines, Miles gives readers a one-of-a-kind survival guide that not only shows the light at the end of the tunnel, but how the journey through the tunnel can be just as shimmering.

Miles's candid voice—full of youthful energy—has made his coming out and transition story accessible to those who may be unfamiliar with the trans experience. The enigmatic spirit I found within minutes of meeting him shines through in all of his online content, and now in this book. Miles's mission is helping those who might be questioning their sexual orientations and/or gender identities—enabling them to find hope in times of the dark unknown. I wish I had had Miles Mckenna in my life when I was younger. Young, insecure, and closeted Tyler might have been less afraid to be himself after seeing the brave and unwavering confidence that Miles McKenna exudes effortlessly. We were lucky enough to have his videos; and now we're blessed to have his book! Okay, enough gushing from me. ENJOY!

Yours,

Tyler Oakley

INTRO

Hey, what's up, you guys? It's Miles! **I'm a queer, transgender, twenty-something-year-old guy** who tries to be funny on the Internet like probably everyone else you know. But for this book, you can think of me like an older sibling, mentor, fairy godbrother, or, if you're willing, a member of your chosen family. **I want to start this off by getting one thing straight (even if you aren't): You do not need someone's approval or acceptance to be who you are or to be proud of who you are.**

If you're reading this, you might be questioning your gender or sexuality, getting ready to come out, or maybe all or none of the above. You might have family or friends who are experiencing those things, or maybe you're just a curious ally. **But no matter where you're coming from, I'm here to help you through it.**

Now, I'm sure you've all heard the phrase "don't worry, it gets better," and while this is often said with good intentions, for anyone who's ever needed that assurance, it's pretty much the most frustrating thing on the planet to hear. Like, lol OK, *when is it going to get better?* Because that part they were telling me not to worry about? It was pretty bad. All I wanted was a magic day on the calendar when suddenly everything would be right again, or really, right for the first time ever. When would it get better? In six months? Six years? It was even harder to hear because **I didn't have any examples of those happy "better" people to look up to for me to say, "Yeah, OK. It's possible." So, that's who I'm going to try and be for you.**

While I can't tell you your exact magical date, I

can tell you about how I got to mine. Turns out it took exactly two years, two months, and two days (I know, weird) from my coming-out date to when I actually tweeted something cheesy but true:

MILES ✔
@TheMilesMcKenna

I heard "it gets better" years ago and thought it wasn't true. Miles you came out 1/2/15 and it just got better 3/4/17. Hold on kids.

12:54 PM · Mar 4, 2017 · Twitter for iPhone

1.2K Retweets   **6.2K** Likes

I remember feeling such relief after facing so much adversity in my youth for just being myself. The parts of myself that I was vulnerable enough to share with family members were originally ignored or ridiculed. I was called slurs and was told I was going to hell. I slept on friends' couches and the backseat of my car when I didn't feel safe going home. I had even tweeted, "Don't come out, it's not worth it." Why did everyone have to know? And why couldn't I just be like everyone else? I'd spent a good amount of my teen years feeling incomplete and then very alone, so to get to that day when I felt differently, was almost a dream.

The stigma that's laid on LGBTQ+ youth is funny—often we are described as either "troubled and confused" or "delicate snowflakes" who need to stand out. My faith in humanity is never stronger than when I meet a young queer kid.

I'm not sure why being confident in one's identity is a trait some people mock, but I hope those people are able to evolve and be more compassionate. Go off, unsupportive moms and dads!

"I'm not sure why being confident in one's identity is a trait some people mock."

a car! Or you attend your first dance. **We experience so many firsts all while trying to navigate who we are and what we believe in.** Up until our teen years, we're told "you can be whoever you want to be," but to a lot of us, that promise ends up being the biggest scam. Unfortunately, that phrase needs a big asterisk: *Only if whoever you are is cis and straight—you know, "the default." If you're not what many automatically presume you are going to be, that added weight of questioning or hiding who you are makes experiencing all those new adventures and figuring out what's next super challenging and isolating.

When I was in that vulnerable place, I found local and online communities that helped me go from being a stubborn kid who swore they'd never come out, to doing so in front of millions of people on the Internet. **As a result of gaining the confidence to come out, I eventually started touring the United States, sharing my stories and cultivating safe spaces for LGBTQ+ youth.**

By surrounding myself with those who embrace who I am and who I want to be, I was able to go back and foster relationships with family members who at first didn't know how to show support, and **I've found the strength to cut ties with those who don't and won't truly see me.**

Because we need support. All of us. Teenage years are filled with changes. Our bodies are constantly shifting and doing weird things, our interests expand, and we want to be free from our parents' rules and expectations. There's a lot of excitement and with that comes a lot of confusion. Maybe you're given keys to

> *"My queerness has taught me strength, my transness has taught me patience and empathy, and my journey up to this point has shown me that standing up for who you are goes beyond sexuality and gender—it is human."*

My queerness has taught me strength, my transness has taught me patience and empathy, and my journey up to this point has shown me that standing up for who you are goes beyond sexuality and gender—it is human.

We are continually coming out and hoping we are accepted by the majority. Not just you but your parents, your siblings, your teacher, your boss. Everyone encompasses intersecting identities with their race, social class, education level, family dynamic, religion—it's not just about sexuality and gender. Today, if those parts of your identity do not align with everyone else's, we're supposed to proclaim them and hope no one tries to change our truth or shun us completely.

It's a strange concept. **Knowing and living your truth is a superpower, not something to fear.** It's how I can look back and understand why I felt so out of place in my middle school dance attire. Or why finding a new jumble of sounds to be called by feels so right. Or how I can look in the mirror and understand what my true identity looks like. Or how I now know who I want to love.

Making those discoveries is a long process and **it's my hope that this is the survival guide that will get you through it.** Within, I have compiled stories and tips from my sad emo boy teen years to help you kick self-discovery's ass and be 100 percent authentically you! I don't know your story or level of safety. **I'm just going to be for you what other people have been for me: an example of being queer, trans, and happy** in a world that brainwashes us into believing all those things can't exist at once.

Here is how I got out and how you can too!

AUTHOR'S NOTE

Labels, as I have come to understand them, are just tools that we use to define ourselves for other people. To have a sense of belonging or exclusion from a pack. Language is constantly evolving and up for interpretation. What's bigger than a definition is the human experience! Be who you are and do what is natural. The mission of this book is to offer validation. There are so many different ways to be and paths to take to become the person you want to be. What follows comes from my personal experience—my advice stems from the things that helped me on my own personal journey. But I am only an expert at being me. If you define yourself as something that isn't in this book, that's great. Maybe you'll write your own book or make a video on what it means to be you! **However you choose to spread love in this world, give it all you've got just like those before you.** If language has evolved by the time you've read this, or anyone was left out of the conversation, that was not my intention. Feel free to pick up the baton and keep the conversation going!

00221402 03C

LETTING GO OF LABELS

My coming-out story started long before I said the words "Mom, Dad, I'm ____."

As I think it does for all of us. I can see my queerness and transness shining through in videos, notebooks, and relationships long before I had the language to describe what it was that I was feeling. Labels are words we use to define ourselves and describe unique human experience. **I like to think of labels as a secondary tool used in your journey of self-discovery.** When I'm asked "How do I know I'm gay?" or "How do I know I'm trans?" my answer is always to do what feels right and live authentically instead of stress over what label you should cling to.

Labels give a great sense of community during a time when you may feel very excluded from communities you thought you were a part of (your home, your school, your friend group). But it can also put a lot of pressure on defining yourself and being "correct" instead of just being. I know I was royally stressed out in my teen years, wondering if I could be ____ and what that would mean for me since____ isn't an *OK* thing to be. What if I came out and I was "wrong"? **It's OK not to know what you identify as!** Labels have more to do with telling someone else who you are than being proactive in your journey. Let's figure out how you feel on the inside before we try to find a word to put to it for everyone on the outside.

When you're ready and/or interested, there is a glossary in the back (page 202) to define any unfamiliar terms.

MILES FROM HOME

WHAT MY LIFE WAS LIKE BEFORE I CAME OUT

PART ONE

I started making YouTube videos for fun in 2007 when I was eleven years old. I was living in Las Vegas and at that time, there weren't many outside forces trying to change who I was. Though I was born with a stereotypical pink bow on my head, I freely dressed very masculine and was consistently the only "girl" on my sports teams. My friends were all cis boys who I had grown up with since I was in SpongeBob boxer briefs that I'd begged for at Target. They would constantly stick up for me if I was teased for being me. I remember when I was eight years old and with my friends at the playground when another group of boys told me that girls weren't allowed.

I froze; I had never been gender-blocked by someone who looked like me before. It had only happened when the occasional adult and/or teacher would use my feminine name as a reason why I couldn't do something that all my cis male friends were doing. Luckily, I didn't have to say anything because my friend Sterling did. "She's cool," he said nonchalantly. "She's just a boy trapped in a girl's body."

The entire class of boys took a look at me, agreed, and then invited me to play. But I was still frozen. I'd never heard of a boy being trapped in a girl's body before. I now know that sentiment resonates with some of my trans peers as a way to define their experience, while others don't feel that way at all! At the time it scared me, because it meant I was seen as different.

Up until that point I had never thought of myself as being "different." That quickly changed as my family moved from the tight-knit community in Las Vegas to the tube top, lip gloss, tween dreamland of Orange County, California. I was twelve and going into middle school. The clothes that had made me look sporty and tomboyish to my cis/het peers who celebrated masculinity now made me weird and different as I entered my teen years. I was too "boyish" in demeanor to be accepted by any of the girls, but my figure was too "girlish" to let me hang out with boys. Middle school gender roles were cutthroat in my town. My first few months being the new kid were miserable at best. (Emos, where you at?)

"She's cool," he said nonchalantly. "She's just a boy trapped in a girl's body."

> ## "I didn't have the language yet to express why I felt that way."

The Internet turned into my escape. There, I could watch people who were much different than the people I knew in my new home, but were very similar to me, even if I didn't have the language yet to express why I felt that way. Reading blogs by trans teens and watching vlogs made by out and proud adults were fun and comforting. **It's as if they walked to the beat of a drum that no one else in my house but me could hear.**

I was obsessed with watching transition videos online when I was thirteen years old, and I did so entirely in secret. I would watch videos and follow blog posts written by transmasculine kids around the globe and learn about hormone replacement therapy and advancements in surgeries; then I'd follow their voice change updates. Seems like that would have been a red flag indicating a desire to transition, right? Wrong. I would convince myself that I was innocently, yet incredibly, fascinated with transgender issues and I was just a very supportive ally to the trans community. It's always surprising and validating to compare experiences with others in the community because **I'm not alone** in doing this!

In hindsight, and now as a self-aware trans person, my cover story of just being very interested in the T of LGBTQ+ didn't match up since I would, of course, only do research on transmasculine people and not transfeminine. It's as if my denial was a defense mechanism developed out of fear of exclusion.

For years I would garner knowledge about the community and arm myself with tools that I would later apply to my own transition. Watching people socially and medically better themselves in the ways they wanted to, and live their truth at a time when those resources wouldn't have been accessible to me, was incredibly comforting. The saying "hindsight is twenty-twenty" speaks volumes to me in my journey. **Even when I was young and couldn't fully define who I was, I was still finding outlets and representation.**

I want to note that no matter who you look up to or admire—someone giving you validation and language to be yourself—*you are that* for someone else. Community is a never-ending cycle, and your experience holds weight.

Being online meant having access to many queer and trans outlets, but offline, I had to live in the real world and that meant middle school. It's really the ultimate crossover episode of childhood and young adulthood. **Puberty starts and you're either told you are becoming a man or becoming a woman.** School dances and dating push heteronormativity onto us even more. This time was so confusing because it was now expected that the parts of me that were "tomboyish" would be left on the playground and I would automatically blossom into this feminine being. I was constantly questioned by family members why I didn't want to wear makeup or feminine clothing, and my pleas to cut my hair short were answered with a resounding *no*.

There were no longer coed sports teams to join and boys weren't supposed to be my friends. They were supposed to be my dates. I was continually getting in trouble for wearing my hood up or bringing a hat to school to hide my long hair. **Female puberty was also nothing to look forward to. The one thing I did like about these raging hormones was getting acne, as it made me look like the generic teen boys I'd seen on *Degrassi*, who I thought were mad cool.**

Still, I managed to make a few very close friends. Though, spoiler alert, everyone turned out queer as well—big shock there. That saying "birds of a feather flock together" is too real. In my late teens,

I found a larger community of queer and gender-variant youth in my area, and **I used the language I had acquired to express how I was feeling.** On one hand, I was being affirmed by like-minded kids my age, but on the other, I was still a long-haired people pleaser with a cross around my neck. **I owe a lot of my strength to those queer kids** I spent most days and nights with who truly saw me for me. They were the first real-life examples of people who looked on the outside the way that I felt on the inside, and, in my eyes, were OK.

I remember thinking how an anvil didn't drop on any of their heads when they cut their hair or when two boys held hands, or if someone changed their name. **And if they could do it, "it" being whatever felt right, then so could I. But first I had to figure out what my "it" was.**

Transreads.org has hundreds of free reading material written by and/or about trans people. Whether you're looking for fictional representation in a book or answers to medical questions in a zine, there are many handpicked by others in the community to choose from. Go to transreads.org!

I'M QUESTIONING MY SEXUALITY. HOW DO I KNOW IF I'M LGBTQ+?

If I could go back in time, I would shake teenage Miles out of obsessively questioning his sexuality. My advice seems so simple now, though at the time, **I had no idea how to navigate my potential queerness.** It's easy to fall into the trap of fear when you're unsure if your identity is different from what you originally thought. I was so scared of what coming out would mean to the people closest to me, and that fear caused me to push down those feelings and later obsessively try to define what I was. **The fear that overwhelmed me once I started to connect the dots of my identity was huge.** I watched movies with gay lovers in secret and followed dozens of accounts of people who embraced queerness. But was I gay? Was I pansexual? Was it a phase? What if I have a coming-out and I'm wrong?

"But was I gay? Was it a phase? What if I have a coming-out and I'm wrong?"

TIPS TO DISCOVERING YOUR SEXUALITY

The best advice I could give to baby me is:

#1 SLOW DOWN. Pay attention young, maybe gay, grasshopper. You don't need to have all the answers about who you are and what you identify as today. And knowing who you are doesn't mean you need to proclaim it tomorrow. Those coming-out fears are so valid, and we will cross that bridge when we get there. Right now we need to find what our truth is. That is something that is yours, and you get to choose the speed of your process. My big advice after years of questioning and then years of being a big gay meme is (drum roll, please), **be mindful of your uncertainty and desire as you move through life**, start dating, and begin finding what feels right (throws confetti).

That's it. That's the whole advice. I think at **the root of sexuality is your unique definition of how you love and how you want to be loved.** In a world where we are told by others what love needs to look like, we can lack the language to define it or be too scared to try and find it. If you think you may like feminine folk, that's great! Maybe you'll meet someone you'll want to ask out on a date. Are you sure you like masculine humans, but you've never dated anyone? Sweet, maybe you'll meet a dude who's totally queer and totally into you! **Everyone's relationship with dating and with themselves is different.** Knowing your truth and your interests and disinterests is more important than contemplating "what ifs" and trying to make a label fit. **My advice to someone questioning their sexuality is to keep living your** life at your own pace and your questions will be answered with time, not with stressing and self-loathing. Before I even had the language to describe how I felt, I was engulfed by the fear of "what if" to the point of pushing away a lot of people and a lot of adventures. This is your story you are writing and no one else's! **Keep moving forward!**

#2 CONTINUE TO LIVE YOUR LIFE.

(Once you've gained some knowledge and the language to define it.) Celebrate this newfound knowledge of your interest or disinterest in other humans and apply it when needed. **Maybe you'll want to have a formal coming-out and share this information with others. Maybe you'll just want to share it with close friends.**

Or maybe you're not ready to share, and that is also totally OK!

Go at your own pace! Self-discovery doesn't mean you need or will have all the answers immediately. Picture this: Fifteen-year-old, gawky Miles, who was definitely wearing a dress, definitely uncomfortable, but who had swallowed those feelings for the sake of trying to fit in, standing awkwardly at a party. At the time, my unknown trans ass was seen as a girl when I was asked, "If you were gay, who would you be with from our school?"

At this point, I hadn't connected all the dots to my identity, but of course, I had an answer immediately. I said I would like this girl (who I "didn't") who was in the grade above me, and that she always talked to me in the halls between classes (but I "didn't even care" since I "wasn't gay"). *Psshhh!* Fast forward to a year later, when we both have the same extracurricular activity together (I'm an overachiever), she comes out as bi and tells me "I wish you liked girls" and was now my next-door neighbor. LET THAT SINK IN. **If there is a god, she must love romantic comedies.**

Now, I know what you're thinking (no, actually, I don't): This was possibly the best thing to happen in my sad, awkward teenage life. I had been practically handed the opportunity to be gay after questioning if I had the gay. The end of a rainbow must have been at my locker, and I was about to get my pot of gold. I had questioned if

I was gay, and here was my chance! But, believe me when I tell you that I still need to find this girl and apologize because we never became protagonists in a gay teen drama since I ran for my life. I ghosted her, I ghosted her friends, I walked my dog on a new route just so I wouldn't pass her house.

I was not ready. Let me say that again in a fancy font: I WAS NOT READY. The fear that was instilled in me led me to not be me. That doesn't mean my coming-out never happened—obviously— but at sixteen, I was not ready and that is OK. Not being prepared to come to terms with any part of your identity is fine. **It's OK to be unsure; just do what feels right!** Whether that is identifying with a label or waiting till one finds you after you run away from your confident bisexual neighbor!

Your story is ever changing and something you are writing every day. Years later, I came across another person I had a crush on (big shock there), and this time I wasn't as scared! (Key word *as*.) My fear of labels and coming out was soon replaced with excitement and that a-ha moment of **"YES, I FIGURED IT OUT!"** due to the fact that I was now ready to come out to myself. Something just clicked in me, and I knew my happiness was worth fighting for. A vast contrast to years before! What I want to tell my younger self—that I'm going to tell you—is that when the time is right to come out in any sense of the phrase, you will know. I think a big piece of the puzzle to get to that point is allowing yourself to go on the journey and celebrating little victories. **Self-discovery isn't a race and you will reach the finish line in your own way!**

NAVIGATING FINDING WHO YOU ARE

As a human who has been seen as that straight girl or that gay girl or that straight guy or that gay guy, I can say that **my trans experience has given me incredible amounts of empathy.** I have viewed the world through many lenses. I've also gone through both "female" puberty and—thanks to hormone replacement therapy—"male" puberty. And I've also been viewed by others with so many different labels. Seriously, there was a time during my transition when I could get into four Ubers in the same week, and each driver would see me as something different. And unfortunately, the service was also different each time.

The most important thing is that I know who I am. That's the advice I give to my peers when they tell me they're not being seen in their homes as who they are. **But how do you even know who you are?** It sounds strange, but humans are a unique species: We come into this world without any self-sufficiency at all. In the beginning, we spend months just crying all the time (and sometimes also in our teen years), then we need help learning how to walk and talk and just be human. In a few years, our spirit starts to shine through, and we gravitate toward specific colors, sounds, and people.

The Internet played a vital role in helping me—and so many other kids—unearth the identities we were raised not to see. Typically, the media we consume as children doesn't show a wide range of representation. I was taught by my family, the media, and my peers that boys and girls get crushes on each other

exclusively. So in hindsight, I had a harder time identifying queer feelings of my own at a young age. **The Internet gave me the ability to pop the small bubble of my home, school, and town and gain validation from posts by like-minded strangers.** I guess that's why there's so much push toward having more representation in the media. If we don't see mature versions of ourselves being successful and happy, then how do we know that we can be? It's cool that I've become that for other kids online. I could send out many thank-you cards to Tyler Oakley, Hannah Hart, and many other Internet icons for being there during my years of self-discovery, which, by the way, never stops! Even when I think I understand this whole waking-up-on-a-rock-floating-in-space thing (life), something new happens to make me cringe at my past self. **Through the years, I've had many unlikely teachers:** some queer, straight, survivors, mothers, children, and friends. It takes a village! **There is a lot you can learn**

from people who aren't afraid to be their authentic selves, even if their journey doesn't wholly mirror your own identity. Someone else's strength can give us a silent OK to take control of our own happiness and avoid following the path we are told is already paved for us.

COMING-OUT TIP #1:
COME OUT TO YOURSELF FIRST

In my experience, owning my identity before I shared it with anyone else outside the community made me stronger. If I hadn't wholeheartedly come out to myself first, I likely would have retreated further into the closet after my family reacted poorly to my announcement (sorry, spoiler!). There's a difference between guarding your magic and who you are from potentially unsupportive people and pretending it doesn't exist.

You exist! At times I felt like a ghost around the people who loved me but didn't really see me. I would remind myself how complete I finally felt, even in light of all my fear surrounding my coming out. **Your identity is yours. You can come out when you feel ready.**

"There's a difference between guarding your magic and who you are from potentially unsupportive people and pretending it doesn't exist."

HOW TO COME OUT TO YOURSELF

It took me years before I was able to fully accept and embrace myself. A self that I was raised not to see, and later told to deny. The first time I heard the words that now define me and my chosen family, they were not given to me in a positive, educational way. With the added weight of a world that is not always the most accepting place, even coming out to yourself can be a difficult process!

My advice for younger me would be to find that positive community and experiment with labels or whatever you are drawn toward. Before my big coming-out moments, I found positive representation to educate myself and a safe space in online communities to figure out what felt right for me. I even started confiding in close friends in that community as I started to feel a stronger connection to who I was versus who I was told I should be. Coming out to people who are part of the LGBTQ+ community—even as questioning—helped turn my fears into celebrations and made me feel less alone.

Coming out to yourself looks different for everyone, just like coming out (as a whole) does. **Coming out to myself meant going at my own pace and gathering what I needed to reach self-acceptance no matter what I uncovered.** Growing up, I could easily dismiss crushes and disguise my gender identity under labels like "tomboy." Hiding the truth from others—but also hiding the truth from myself—was familiar and routine . . . until it wasn't.

> ## "So I already had this fear that even if I figured out who I was, someone would try and change me."

I remember when I was sixteen, there was some documentary out about conversion therapy, and I remember asking one of my family members what they would do if I was gay, and they told me that they'd call a priest and "get me help." So I already had this fear that even if I figured out who I was, someone would

try and change me. I told myself that I couldn't be gay. That I didn't feel anything when I kissed guys because I must be asexual. Looking back, it makes sense that it never felt right. I was kissing guys who wanted to be kissing girls! Since I now know that I never fit that description— *girl*—it makes sense why those interactions never felt right. Now that I am seen as me—a guy—the act of dating guys, girls, and nonbinary people doesn't feel out of place because I'm finally being seen as me by everyone I date. **Once I came out to myself and fully stepped into my identity, I didn't care what adversity or hurdles I would face, even though deep down I knew that I might face many.**

I remember one summer after coming out to myself, writing in my iPhone notes that anything bad would be worth the good. That my teenage queer crush was worth fighting for. **It was as if the universe was handing me a letter that said, "Here you go. You can feel love. This is what it's supposed to feel like."** Not that I was in love with anyone specific, but this was the first time I was facing a part of my identity and wasn't running from it or trying to call it by another name. Allowing myself to be me within the safety of my friend group/online blog posts let me see all the parts of me that had been hiding, and that experience told me it would be OK. Basically, having a supportive community and chosen family during this vulnerable time gave me the armor to endure the possible negative reactions that coming out to everyone could hold.

Ignorance and hate have touched me as a member of the LGBTQ+ community. However, I possess a lot of privilege. I am male. I am white. I have been given

incredible opportunities, like writing this book.

Through these pages you'll find little history blurbs from some individuals whose activism and art inspired me (outside of history class!). I hope you connect with them as well! These people have all contributed to making the community and world a safer place for many intersecting identities.

IFTI NASIM (1946–2011) was a Pakistani American poet who published gay Urdu poetry, which was the first queer love–themed piece to ever be published in that language. His art and truth aided in the fight to dismantle homophobia in Pakistan. There is power in honesty and love!

MILES'S NEW TEN COMMANDMENTS:

IF GOD CAN MAKE RULES IN HER BOOK SO CAN I!

#1 YOU DON'T NEED TO WEAR A MASK TO FIND ACCEPTANCE.

#2 GROWING AND CHANGING IS PART OF LIFE!

#3 PEOPLE REACT POORLY TO SITUATIONS OUT OF FEAR, AND FEAR COMES FROM THE UNKNOWN.

#4 UGLY AND BEAUTIFUL LOOK DIFFERENT TO EVERY PERSON. WEAR WHAT FEELS RIGHT TO YOU.

#5 YOU ARE VALID IN YOUR IDENTITY, EVEN IF YOU'RE THE ONLY ONE WHO CAN DEFINE IT.

#6 THE MOST IMPORTANT RULE IN LIFE IS TO BE KIND TO YOURSELF AND OTHERS. AS LONG AS YOU DO THAT, YOU'RE GOLDEN.

#7 LISTEN TO YOUR BODY AND PUT YOUR MENTAL HEALTH FIRST!

#8 EVERYONE'S COMING-OUT PROCESS LOOKS DIFFERENT.

#9 FIND YOUR OUTLET TO EXPRESS YOURSELF AND CULTIVATE FRIENDSHIPS WITH LIKE-MINDED PEOPLE.

#10 YOU ARE ALLOWED TO TAKE UP SPACE.

MILES OUT OF THE CLOSET

HOW I CAME OUT AND HOW YOU CAN TOO

COMING OUT AS QUEER

When I was freshly nineteen, I had what I consider as my first ever coming-out experience—I'm not counting friends who were queer or people in the community who I'd already told—with one of my parents. Months after I acknowledged

was questioned in a soft way that made what I had assumed was an unsupportive home feel like a safe space after all. Maybe I had been wrong, and I could come out. In my mind, the discovery of my identity was the best thing to happen to me, and

> "Months after I acknowledged to myself that I was gay, one of my parents asked me what the deal was."

to myself that I was gay, one of my parents asked me what the deal was. (It was worded a little differently.) Since I had been feeling more comfortable in myself, I had become less willing to dress femininely for others' approval and I had an ever-changing iPhone wallpaper of gay icons. (This was what tipped them off!) I didn't go into that night armed with rehearsed words as weapons and ready to come out. I

I believed (and still do) that every parent fundamentally wants their kid to be happy.

My exact words were, "I like guys, but I like some girls too." Those were the words I had at the time, and they were mixed with a lot of fear and anxiety. I started to cry. Whether they were tears of relief or sadness, I don't know. I remember arms wrapping around me and being hugged so sweetly with words in my ear saying, "I will always love you."

And let's pause here because this was the biggest shock. I just need you to know that this loving response had been unimaginable from this particular family member. Years before, in my home state of California, that parent had voted yes on the proposition against gay marriage! The attitude toward LGBTQ+ people or groups in my household would, at times, be very negative. But with that hug, every ounce of fear left my body.

We had been holding each other for some time when they said, with me still in their arms, "But you're still going to hell." Now, my dumbass started laughing. I felt so much relief because I thought they were joking! I thought this was going so well, we could even make jokes on the first day! If you follow me online, then you know this is my sense of humor. Also, if you follow me online, then you know this was not a joke. As I was laughing with tears of joy in my eyes, I was taken out of the embrace and sternly told, "No, I'm serious."

Up until that point, I had never had a movie moment where everything went black, and I couldn't hear or see. My parent began to recite Bible verses and I completely sank into myself. Mind you, I didn't think I had been raised in an especially religious household before my coming-out experience. I believe it was the fear of LGBTQ+ being a sin and the religious ideals that had been instilled in them during their childhood that made

them believe I was going against God, and ultimately going to hell. After that initial embrace, they reacted to my coming out with anger, disbelief, and hurtful words.

Of course, this is all from my point of view, since our communication from then on was hostile and, eventually, nonexistent. **Because we can only experience the world through our own perspectives, we all tend to view ourselves as the protagonist to any story.** Just as I thought family members were wrong to try to change me, they thought the LGBTQ+ community was wrong and trying to harm their child. Though it may not seem like it, I believe that in my situation—as well as the situations of others who I am close to—love mixed with fear can be mistaken as hate.

I was then told I had to come out to my other parent under threat of being kicked out of our home because it could potentially hurt their marriage if I didn't. **This was when I was also forced to grow up and learn healthy coping skills, communication tools, and how to rely on myself.** I felt like my identity was no longer mine. Instead it was something to be ashamed of, changed, and put out in the open for a public display. That's what it felt like when I was made to tell someone before I was ready.

I told my other parent, this time in public to, you know, spice things up. (Maybe if I was in a restaurant, I wouldn't bawl my eyes out!) I was wrong. I started it off by saying, "I have something to tell you." There was no turning back after that. (Wow, is this hard to write about!) I

"Love mixed with fear
can be mistaken as hate."

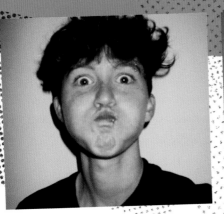

muttered the same words I had before, and here's what I got back: "Our relationship will never be the same." The statement was very true. **At the time, that seemed like the end of the world, but looking back, I am so thankful for that truth. (Hint, hint: "It gets better.")**

Many LGBTQ+ people struggle with feeling pressure to choose either their identity or their spirituality. Though that wasn't my journey, if that's yours, you don't have to choose one part of yourself—you can celebrate it all. There are many LGBTQ+ churches and places of worship you can get involved with! I recently interviewed a gay pastor from Founders Metropolitan Community Church Los Angeles, which has had a long history of inclusion and acceptance since opening in the sixties—as well as many queer pastors leading sermons! Gaychurch.org is a site where you can find an LGBTQ+ friendly church near you.

LIVING IN GAY PURGATORY

After coming out and having it not go well, living under the same roof with my family was strange. My relationship with them changed dramatically. It felt like my entire world had caved in on itself because no one looked at me the same way anymore. In my eyes, the only thing that had changed was how comfortable I now felt in my own skin and how self-aware I was about who I wanted to be with, but some family members didn't see it like that. I was pretty much thrown into gay purgatory where I was technically out, but it wasn't OK.

I kept thinking, *If I'm with a guy, then I'd be accepted.* That type of thinking is so harmful for a teenager—or anyone. It was as if I wasn't worthy of love and, if I could only be someone I wasn't, everything would be OK. I started to try to compromise my own truth once again

in order to find acceptance. **Ultimately, I learned that I have to be true to myself and I'm worthy of love exactly the way I am.**

That's the battle I was fighting. I was navigating this push and pull of fully knowing what was expected of me and what I thought people wanted for me, while also undeniably knowing who I was and what was going to make me the happiest and the most me. I spent the next eight months figuring out how to BE after everything was out in the open and unwelcomed. **The desire to be who you are and the desire to be with those you love is a crossroads I never want another kid to have to encounter.** Eventually, I started to feel a sense of contentment inside that I didn't realize I could, but the people I loved weren't willing to go on that journey with me.

So then what? Did I cut my hair, stop hiding my gay texts, and be fully me? Or did I go further into the closet than ever before? Vote now on your smartphones! We all know the answer, but honestly, the second option was very tempting. I started being me, no matter what anyone had to say about it. And over time I stopped being so afraid of it. By slowly accepting my truth in terms of attraction and sexuality, other parts of my identity began to fall into place. I started unapologetically dressing more masculinely and being more confident in social situations because I knew my truth and I knew I could hold space. I wasn't alone.

The fear of my relationships with my parents changing was unlike any other coming-out experience I had in my adolescence. As I'm older now, my relationships with family members have continued to grow and shift. Advice I would give from one kid who's come out

> "So then what? Did I cut my hair, stop hiding my gay texts, and be fully me? Or did I go further into the closet than ever before?"

59

> ## "Every argument with family seemed like the end of the world to my teenage brain."

to another is: As you grow, relationships will evolve with you. Just like my fears of defining myself seemed catastrophic, every argument with family seemed like the end of the world to my teenage brain. By looking back—and being an aggressive optimist—I learned valuable lessons (including the depths of my independence and the conviction I felt in my identity) through hard conversations with family members who didn't get it.

My YouTube channel quickly became my safe space and played a vital role in allowing me to take control of my happiness. **Because of the Internet, I could communicate with hundreds of thousands of other edgy teens who loved the part of me that (it felt like) people close to me were ashamed of.** But it was so much more than Internet clout; it was hope. My hobby turned into a vital lesson that taught me there are so many people in the world, and it's better to find like-minded ones than to wear a mask and earn approval.

HOW TO COPE WHEN YOU'RE LIVING WITH THOSE WHO DON'T ACCEPT YOU

Having pride in who you are amidst ignorance or negativity is something everyone navigates differently! Maybe you're at an unsupportive school or job or you're living under the same roof with people who choose not to see what you see. When I was in that place, I found outlets through making videos, writing, and surrounding myself with my community. I also started reading a lot, both about LGBT history as well as people in other communities going on their own journeys of self-discovery.

Reading inspired me to live life like I'm living a story. Basically, make your life story the one you want to read. This helped me channel negative feelings into positive work to get the life that I wanted. **I chose to make my story about working hard (even if it was at part-time jobs), building my community on** YouTube and offline, and being the most genuine version of myself that I could be no matter what.

BAYARD RUSTIN (1912–1987) was a gay civil rights leader who fought for social justice. He's famously remembered as the lead organizer of the 1963 March on Washington, a march held to protest racial discrimination and to advocate for the rights of African Americans. Equality for intersecting identities!

LEAVING HOME

In my late teens, I was living in a constant limbo where being myself meant having a strong desire to live on my own, but it was never the "right time" to take that step. Never enough money in my pockets or never enough wind in my sails. None of my friends had left their parents' homes yet. Even the ones who chose to go to college all chose schools close enough to continue living under their parents' roofs. Attending college was a choice that was never decided for me or forced on me by my family, and I am very thankful for that.

Migrating out of the house on my own sounded pretty in queer movies, but very confusing in real life. It wasn't until a famous traveling circus came into town that I saw a way out! (I'm not kidding.) For a few weeks, I fell into a cast of circus folk who accepted my queerness, and I had a job opportunity that allowed me to travel the country. It was like something out of a fairy tale and something that, in hindsight, is very "me."

Unfortunately, I don't have any wild tales of living life on a train and

befriending clowns. I saw this wacky opportunity as a way to leave home, but also as a way to run away. At the time, I was working multiple part-time jobs and slowly coming out to everyone I worked with. The story I wanted to write for myself involved living in Los Angeles and cultivating a space for queer kids like myself on the Internet—*not* living on a train or continuing to beg for more hours at retail jobs, which I'd historically taken out of necessity and not passion. **I realized the "right moment" I was looking for didn't exist, but the community and chosen family I had been gathering did!** With the help of my community, I set out to live the life I wanted.

What I learned from this confusing— yet exciting—time in my life is that with fear paralyzing you, it will never seem like the right time to do a lot of things. There will never be enough money, or courage, or friends in the area, or places for rent . . . the list goes on. That fear of the unknown and that comfort in familiarity—no matter how uncomfortable the circumstances may be—can keep us from doing a lot of things in our lives.

My exit from my parents' home was pretty abrupt once I came to that conclusion. After a big fight with a family member when I was continuously told to feel grateful that I hadn't been kicked out, I knew it was time to leave. Whether or not my bank account was ready, I had to go in order to continue to grow into the person I was meant to be. Luckily I had friends and a community to lean on during this in-between period of figuring out how to live on my own. **(If you or anyone you know are at risk of homelessness and are LGBTQ+, there are many organizations out there that were created to help.** My Friends Place is an LA-based organization that offers necessities and skill-building programs for homeless LGBTQ+ youth. For more information go to myfriendsplace.org.) Leaving was incredibly hard to do, as my bonds with other family members had started to grow stronger, and my absence definitely hurt those relationships—but it was an inevitable event.

I was initially afraid to tell any of my friends since I didn't want to be a burden. (There goes that pesky vulnerability again!) I'm grateful that I

> "That fear of the unknown and that comfort in familiarity can keep us from doing a lot of things in our lives."

was incredibly optimistic about the entire situation. No matter if the day was good or bad, it was mine, because I was being 100 percent me.

There are great TED Talks by Brené Brown about vulnerability and shame going hand in hand that gave me a new perspective. Asking for help or for a spotlight on you can feel like a mountain

my audience would accept me. I was just documenting that, because I came out and the environment was no longer sustainable for my growth, I wasn't living with Mom and Dad anymore. Video-making is like a two-way street: Just as online strangers found validation from my posts, I found community and strength in those people. I was taking everyone on a

> "Asking for help or for a spotlight on you can feel like a mountain in the middle of your journey."

in the middle of your journey. I was incredibly vulnerable when a close friend asked—on the night I decided to leave my parents' place—the daunting question, "How are you?" It's funny how rarely we genuinely answer that question, considering how often we hear it. The person asking was none other than YouTube sensation and a recent member of my chosen family, Stevie Boebi.

YouTube, at that point, was still a hobby. My first "coming-out" video online wasn't me baring my soul and hoping

journey with me and looking for a friendly face in a sea of profile pictures, instead of fearing that I wouldn't be accepted. (That's the positive to vulnerability, people!)

Creating videos online wasn't a job for me at the time, but it was for Stevie! She took me in and was a role model for me in many ways. She taught me how to be out, how to live on my own, and how to make being a YouTuber my job. **Asking for help led me to great mentors and valuable lessons!**

COMING-OUT TIP #2:
MAKE SURE YOU ARE IN A SAFE ENVIRONMENT

Q: What is a safe environment?

A: It's a space where your coming-out is not met with hostility that can lead to homelessness or any form of abuse.

Q: How do you know if your environment isn't safe?

A: If LGBTQ+ topics are brought up in your home and they're met with aggression rather than tolerance or acceptance, your environment may not be safe.

Are you coming out to a family member you are dependent on for food or shelter?

Are you coming out in a workplace and discrimination could render you jobless?

Are you secure and prepared for things not to go in your favor or is it better to be selective about who you tell at this moment?

Everyone's coming-out process is different, and sometimes waiting until you are in a safe space to communicate your identity is necessary. The most important thing is that you are aware of your truth and know how to take control of your own happiness.

SOME POSSIBLE NEGATIVE REACTIONS THAT MAY ARISE WHEN YOU COME OUT:

Some people may feel hurt that they weren't told sooner or betrayed, as though you have been lying to them.

Some people will act emotionally (with tears, shock, or anger).

Some family members might mourn the loss of a life they had envisioned for you.

Some people may see your identity as a sin or an act against their religious beliefs.

Some parents may be misinformed that LGBTQ+ people can't have families or lead successful lives. They may react defensively and try to "protect you."

Some people may act in anger and denial because of judgments they have about the community.

> "Sometimes people close to us also need a period of time to learn about different identities, just like we did."

Some negative reactions require time to process until things get better! It may have taken you months or even years before you felt comfortable with a label or even your identity! **Sometimes people close to us also need a period of time to learn about different identities, just like we did.** In a world that brainwashes us into thinking we are born with default identities, there may be a necessary period of unlearning. By now you've had time to get used to who you are—give the people close to you that same space to get to know the new you.

If you plan to come out, you get to choose the who and the where! There is no rule that your truth has to be on blast for everyone all at once. And there are precautions you can take to make sure you have ample support before you make that leap. **Tell close friends/people in your life who you think will be accepting before telling people you are unsure about.** Before I came out for the first time—even though I didn't plan to come out at that exact moment—I had already told my close friends (as well as adult friends at work)

about my identity. Many people close to me were made aware that my family did not know yet. They also knew about my apprehension about what their reaction would be. This came in handy. I had people to emotionally support me—an emotional safety net—when it didn't go as well as I'd hoped.

COMING OUT AS TRANSGENDER

It took a year out on my own until I came out with my gender identity. **A big thank-you to all the trans kids who said my first videos helped them come out during a time when I was too scared to ever go through that process again.** You can have all the support in the world—and with the combination of my chosen family and my growing Internet family, you could say I did—and still be scared to come out.

The same was true for lots of people I know and that's because there were both external conflicts and internal conflicts working against them. **Even if everyone around you is supportive, you can still feel unsafe or unsure about coming out.** There is so much internalized homophobia and transphobia—often caused by never seeing your identity mirrored on TV, or never seeing public wedding proposals with a relationship that looks like yours, or maybe hearing someone in public office say something negative about your label—that it's not only hard to come out to unsupportive people, but it can also be hard to come out to supportive people if you are not ready.

After I moved to LA, I had a bunch of out queer friends, as well as "allies" who happened to be closeted LGBTQ+ members. I watched them come out to all of us through the years, just blocks from West Hollywood, the gay capital of Los Angeles. On the surface, they shouldn't have been afraid because we were all queer, though some friends still cried when they told me they were bi. It's OK to be afraid of coming out. **Everyone's journey is different, and everyone's way of internalizing that journey ranges as well.** You can't live life by comparison, only by following your truth. No matter who you are, fear of the unknown is OK. Fear of vulnerability is OK.

I continued exploring my truth when I was twenty-one and came out as transgender. **I went from being that self-aware kid to that awkward people-pleasing teen to an adult with one foot planted firmly on *I don't give a fuck* and the other on *this is me.*** I made the announcement with a video on my YouTube channel, right before my first nationwide tour, that said I was transgender and planned to change my name as a part of my transition.

This was a huge deal, as all of my usernames that I'd had for a decade were about to change, and I needed hundreds of thousands of people to address me correctly. A lot of weight there! But my fear of not being accepted wasn't greater than the feeling of knowing who I was and how I wanted to be seen. **A quote that I repeated during that time and still live by is "I'd rather be hated for who I am, than loved for who I am not."**

Fortunately, I had an overwhelming amount of support from my audience and was able to meet a lot of them on tour soon after. I didn't realize it at the time, but I didn't get misgendered or dead-named once through my seventeen-city tour. **Kids, teens, and parents showed me nothing but support, and I will be forever grateful for this expanded family.** The coming-out experience I most anticipated at the time was with the one parent whom I still

had a relationship with. This coming-out was so much different from the last one. I often think that if my first coming-out experience had gone as well as my second, I would've graduated into my current self a lot sooner and would not have been stifled by all the "what ifs" for as long as I was.

"Coming out sucked. I'm never doing that again!" said I, the person who totally needed to come out again. I sat my parent down (in public again, ROUND TWO) and explained the changes and my feelings behind them. **This time, after a few years of mixed emotions, time, and more and more communication, I was met with a smile and a simple, "OK."** THAT WAS IT. We had tears in our eyes,

but not the sad kind, and I asked if that was it. They said, "You're still my child, right?" (Quick applause for character development!) **This time I was met with love.** It took a lot of vulnerability, communication, and eventually acceptance to get there . . . and we got there! A prime example of some people just needing time.

> "It took a lot of vulnerability, communication, and eventually acceptance to get there . . ."

COMING-OUT TIP #3:
IT'S OK TO IDENTIFY AS SOMETHING ELSE LATER

If you feel a certain way now, but in the future, you no longer connect with that specific label, that is fine! Good advice I once heard on a queer/gender panel I was on with lesbian and LGBT activist Steph Frosch was that identities are a lot like shoe sizes. I used to be a size four, but now I'm a size seven. I needed to be a size four first to get to my final shoe size, but my current identity isn't invalidated by the route I took to get here. **If your label changes, it doesn't mean you were wrong; it means you were still growing.** From the time I heard Steph's

A message to parents: If your kid, no matter their gender, wants to kiss a girl, they should be allowed to be with the people they are attracted to. If your kid wants to wear a hoodie instead of a skirt, they should be allowed to dress the way they want to. They're following their journey, and whether it leads to an LGBTQ+ label or not, it's something only they can discover. But giving them their space to grow into their "shoe sizes" will only make their journey that much more positive.

I first came out as gay before I came

> "If your label changes, it doesn't mean you were wrong; it means you were still growing."

words to now, I have grown into myself as well! At the time I didn't have the words for my gender identity—only my sexuality. I was able to come out again once I grew into my shoe size, and so can you!

out as a queer guy with a trans experience. There's no right or wrong journey, but it's the one I lived.

You don't need to be afraid of the journey, because it will lead you to who you are meant to be.

"What if my label changes?" is a question that keeps a lot of us up at night. Weighing the options of "Should I come out?" against "What if it changes?" Back in 2017, I interviewed Aydin Olsen-Kennedy, a gender therapist and executive director at the Los Angeles Gender Center. It is a nonprofit that works with gender non-conforming and transgender communities and refers them to psychologists, family therapists, and many more vital resources. If you're Trans or Questioning and in the Los Angeles area, go to LAGenderCenter.org!

Something Aydin said that stuck with me was that you can't know exactly how you'll feel about something until you get there. Worries and what ifs are so valid, but they are bridges we will cross together when and if they come up. **For me, and for many other trans people, my sexuality changed a lot after I started transitioning.** The first label I ever came out with was "gay." At the time, I was being seen as a girl, but never used the term "lesbian." It makes a lot of sense now why a feminine term didn't feel right to me. After I came out as trans and started socially transitioning, I also started dating more than just girls! I was finally being seen as me.

Since feeling 100 percent me and being seen as such, I've felt an immeasurable boost of confidence and have dated all types of people. So my label DID change as I got older, which is totally fine. And if I hadn't had the journey I did, I'm not sure I would've figured everything out in the same way. **Listen to who you are and where you are right now and live authentically!** As long as you are honest with yourself, you are on the right path.

AUDRE LORDE (1934–1992) was, in her own words, a "black, lesbian, mother, warrior, poet." She celebrated diversity in her poems and combated racism and homophobia with art. Share who you are through whatever medium you work in, and you can elicit change!

GUIDE TO COMING OUT

When I'm asked how I knew I was ready to come out, my answer is always, "I felt like I was done cooking." It was as if a timer went off in my head and I was ready to be fully me in every area of my life and to every person. In terms of my sexuality, I was very secure in who I was attracted to, but there had been an empty feeling at times since I couldn't express my happiness to everyone close to me. **As for my gender identity, I was sure I'd cracked the code on who I was and needed to let others know as part of my transition to feeling 100 percent me.**

The expression "coming out of the

closet" is spot on because I'd definitely felt alone and hidden up to that point. Even though it wasn't all rainbows and sunshine when I came out, it was still my decision. **Don't feel pressured to come out if you are not ready or you're not sure if the environment you're in is safe.** I spent a long time guarding myself and letting in a few trusted allies before I opened that door. Coming out is a part of your journey, and everyone's process is different.

A few years ago, I was hosting a meet and greet in Montana. I met a kid who was fourteen and terrified to come out. They told me about a girlfriend they had been seeing in secret and their journey coming to terms with their sexuality. I commended them on having the confidence to be themself at such a young age even if members of their family didn't know. They expressed their fears—what might people may say if they came out? It was a typical tale of gay fear in the twenty-first century.

After some time, they go, "Maybe it will be OK . . ." (1 point for coach Miles) ". . . my dad is transgender, and my mom is pretty queer, but I just don't want things to be weird, you know." My jaw dropped to the floor, and I just laughed. I gave them a hug and assured them that I thought they were going to be OK. That's only one example. I've met teens in tears who were afraid to come out as trans to their gay parents, gay kids afraid to be out in a world full of prejudiced people, and bisexual friends afraid to come out to me! **Coming out is scary no matter the circumstances!** No matter how it looks on the outside, you don't know what another person is going through. No one's situation is better or worse than another, everyone internalizes experiences differently and is on their own schedule. **Respect your friends who have yet to come out and respect yourself if you need more time as well.**

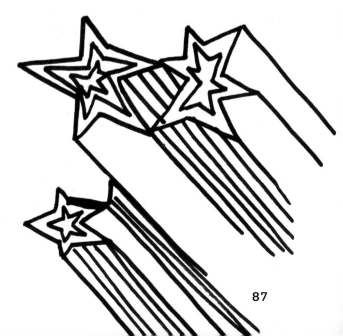

COMING-OUT CONVERSATION STARTERS

Before I came out, I imagined it'd be like the small amount of fictional gay content I'd seen on TV shows (that were clearly made by straight people). **It would be a big movie moment where I'd bare my soul to a crowd and I'd either be unanimously accepted or rejected.** In reality, it's more like a Dr. Seuss book. I came out here, I went out there. I came out in a tree, I came out to a bee. If you choose to come out, you may have to do it quite a few times, so here are some conversation starters to get you going!

#1 "I have something I need to tell you." A classic. Something I used since there's little wiggle room to back out after those words are uttered.

#2 "Gay! I mean, hey! But also gay, I'm gay." Not subtle, but also not incorrect.

#3 "Bi!" This can be said when exiting a room or event. May need additional clarification if used for coming out.

#4 "Guess what I figured out the other day! I like ____." Girls? Boys? A name of someone of a specific gender? It's casual, it's honest, it's out!

#5 "Can I have the bathroom pass? Also, the correct pronouns?" A ballsy move if made during class.

#6 Pointing at something that isn't straight followed by a trendy, "Me" or, "Wow, same."

#7 Showing up to a straight function in full rainbow attire.

#8 "You know who's cute? [Insert name of cutie.]" I mean, it's true, it doesn't have to be so deep!

#9 Literally saying anything on April first just in case it goes horribly wrong because you can always be like, "Pfffft—You thought!"

#10 "My girlfriend/boyfriend/partner also likes true crime documentaries!" I would say shit like this all the time even when I was single! Just to make sure my peers knew I had the gay. Very nonchalant, yet very affirming when you don't know how to tell an acquaintance!

COMING OUT TO YOUR GRANDPARENTS!

Maybe I just come from a bloodline that is full of acceptance but it skipped a generation, or perhaps with old age comes an attitude of peace toward things that don't concern you. Either way, my coming-outs with both sets of extended relatives were a breeze! One side of my family was elated that I now felt comfortable in my own skin and they had so many questions about my love life and journey of self-discovery. **I told them over the phone and remembered my grandma shouting, "LGBT IS HERE TO STAY!"**

Other relatives wanted to trade stories of their own queer youth experiences and had an attitude toward sexuality that was rooted in just being human and not being different. You can never judge a book by its cover! Old age doesn't always mean old ideas; it can also mean being old enough to know that you have to live your truth. Celebrating differences can happen at any age! This doesn't mean that coming out to your grandparents is going to be the same as it was for me, but I would just say, don't go into it with preconceived notions.

"Old age doesn't always mean old ideas; it can also mean being old enough to know that you have to live your truth."

I carried those fears and assumptions for a while because coming out to my parents didn't go well. I didn't want to allow myself to be vulnerable again. **To use a Disney princess analogy, I was very Ariel—silent—when I wished I could have been Mulan.** Actually, I would have rather been Li Shang or Prince Eric, but you get the idea. This is a common feeling that I see in many kids who message me for support.

Sometimes when you come out, it's like you're a ghost in your own home. Life goes on, and you're treated like nothing ever happened, an erasure of the truth so people around you can preserve the person they think of as you. Or sometimes you're the topic of a very negative discussion, and it feels like anything you say drags you further into the quicksand of disappointment.

Going back to my bitch, Ariel. My

silence offered another lesson I'd take with me beyond the walls of my parents' house: People react poorly to things out of fear, and fear comes from the unknown. **When I'm asked by fans what I would do differently if I had to come out again, I always say I would've written a book.** Not necessarily a book like this, but a notebook filled with all the things I was too afraid to say.

I had so many stories I wanted to share, but too much gay fear to say anything at all. My notebook would have had links to videos of people who could explain what I was going through better than I could at the time. I'd list successful people who identify similarly to me to show positive representation that my family might not be aware of. **I believe a lot of negative attitudes I faced came from a lack of information.** I think I was surrounded by people who had a lot of propaganda thrown at them in their youths (during the AIDS epidemic) and lack queer representation among friends and acquaintances now, in their adulthood. I think a lot of people lose the chance to have awesome relationships with their LGBTQ+ relatives because of this lack of positive and accurate representation. As a person coming out, it's hard to be the one to give all this needed information to those around you. When my coming out initially didn't go well, it was hard to imagine opening up even more. **If I had to do it over again, I would have written down resources my loved ones could have utilized.** Doing so would have allowed me to speak up, protect my mental health, and plant the seed for potential growth in our communication.

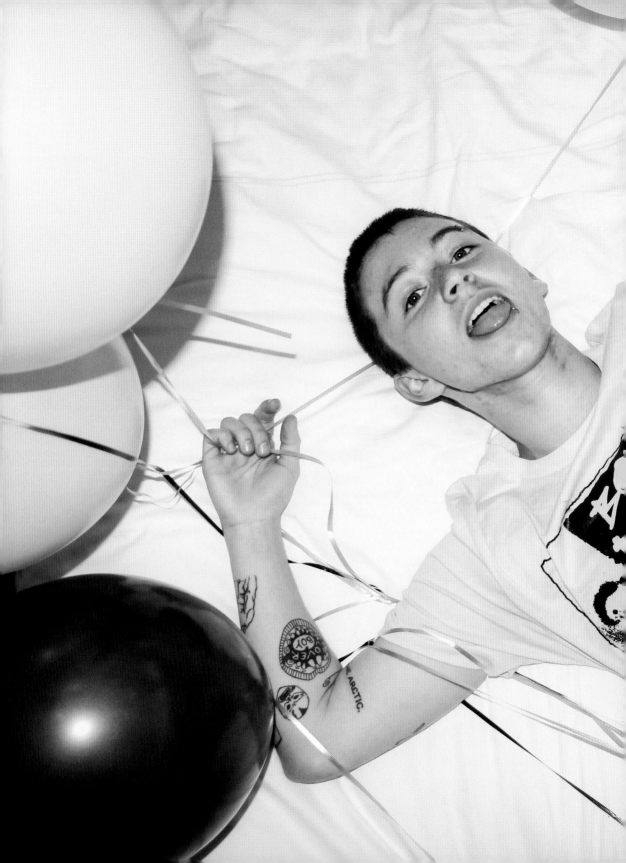

HOW TO CREATE YOUR OWN COMING-OUT BOOK

This can be given or read to someone, or can be a therapeutic activity to better connect with yourself! You don't owe anyone answers or need their approval to validate your existence. **You are allowed to take up space, you are allowed to love, you are allowed to feel safe and content in your own skin—without approval from anyone.** If you want to let someone close to you understand your identity but the thought of talking face-to-face fills you with anxiety, write it down! **Writing down your coming-out experience can give you a chance to pick and choose what you want to say without the fear of not saying it at all.** It also provides the reader with an opportunity to digest the information you've given them instead of reacting emotionally or with judgment.

ESSENTIAL GEAR

A notebook

Texting or typing works, but adults typically find higher sentiment in something handwritten—don't ask me why. This theory can be easily viewed when looking at the difference in the enthusiasm they give you after receiving a birthday card versus a birthday text. Plus, something permanent like ink on a page can be referred back to and not quickly deleted.

Here are some questions to get you started:

What labels do you cling to?

What do these labels mean to you?

Who are some people you identify with? Is there any media they've produced that you can share? Music that you connect with? A video or movie?

What are your goals for the future relating to your identity? Do you want to see a gender therapist? Do you need permission to go to a dance with someone?

What felt out of place in your life before you realized how you identify?

Then think about how the reader can best support you. In a perfect world, what would you like to happen? Do you want anything to change? Do you want them to be engaged and go to a pride event/center with you? Do you need them to use a new name or pronouns for a social transition? **Instead of wishing someone would do something, sometimes it's helpful to name exactly what you need to feel supported so they can try to meet you there!**

During my first coming out, I wasn't able to open a dialogue about my teenage love stories, like the time I stopped traffic to ask a girl for her number after she screamed a compliment at my rainbow hat. Or the first time I took a girl out on a date, and, embarrassingly, it just happened to be Valentine's Day. **Authentic experiences that are rooted in love humanize the coming-out experience.** That's something that's lost in the eyes of frantic parents who are afraid of their child's sexuality—the fact that it's human.

If you feel safe and it's important to you, communicate your journey as well as your identity! I'll go back to my Ariel comparison from earlier (last time, I promise!): The looks of shock, confusion, and disappointment from the people closest to me after I shared my sexuality might as well have been Ursula the sea witch swooping down to steal my voice. The whole point of having a coming-out is to have communication, but with the threat of losing people closest to you, that can feel impossible to do. For me, it actually was impossible since many parts of my story went unsaid even up until now. If a coming-out book can be your way to let it all out for others or even just for yourself, it's going to be worth it. **Tell your story.**

I now have such a strong relationship with one parent who didn't know how to support me when I first came out but was willing to learn. Through the years, communication from my end was a key factor in teaching them how to communicate with and support me.

"The whole point of having a coming-out is to have communication, but with the threat of losing people closest to you, that can feel impossible to do."

HOW TO FIND YOUR CHOSEN FAMILY

Your chosen family is your community. Whether your identities intersect or you're an ally to one another, these are people you can rely on and open up to. I've found many chosen family members through the years. Here are some ways you can find your own chosen family!

100

1 Get involved in an activity or club outside of the house.

Does your school have a Genders & Sexualities Alliance (GSA—formerly Gay-Straight Alliance) that you feel comfortable joining? Are you interested in any sports or activities like video-making or art that lend themselves to joining a club, team, or a class? Opening up to others can be hard, and during times when I have felt rejection or suffered from low self-esteem, I've been known to shut myself out from the world and not take part in group activities. While time alone to recharge from other people is great for healing, allowing yourself to be involved in a group activity as a part of your weekly routine can let like-minded people enter your space! Because of the Equal Access Act of 1984 a public school cannot deny the formation of a club as a form of discrimination. If your school doesn't have a GSA, consider creating one! Go to gsanetwork.org for more information, training, and support.

2 Find an online community.

Reach out to someone who has shared their story online or share your own in the form of a post or video! Digitally teaming up with community members around the world reminded me just how small my bubble was during my teen years. Before I found other queer kids in my area, I would Skype queer friends in Australia (literally the other side of the world) for hours! If you're not ready to come out yet and don't want your identity intertwined with your social media, there are plenty of safe alternatives! TrevorSpace.org is an online community for LGBTQ+ and Questioning youth ages thirteen to twenty-four. There you can virtually meet other LGBTQ+ peers without fear of bullies or coming out online. There are live forums discussing topics from "How to come out" to "How do you tell your crush you like them?" This is a safe space for you to build community as well as get answers to questions revolving around your identity that you may not have been able to ask!

3 Reconnect with old friends.

In our youth, friends tend to come and go with changing classes, moving, and growing out of relationships. When I realized that I'd grown a lot since a particular point in time, I also realized that it's safe to assume the people I was hanging out with back then have grown as well! Like I said, almost all my friends I grew up with ended up having coming-out experiences too. You never know who around you may be navigating similar territory.

4 Involve yourself with activism and summer programs!

Camp Brave Trails is an LGBTQ+ youth summer camp where you can make friends with varying identities and learn how to be a leader for social good in your area! They have locations for the summer in multiple U.S. cities plus a Family Camp where LGBTQ+ families can come together for a weekend to grow and build community. "A safe and welcoming space for LGBTQ+ Youth." Go to BraveTrails.org!

5 Seek an after-school safe haven!

A quick call to your LGBTQ+ center in your state will give you all the information on what queer youth activities they provide or are near you. For example, in multiple cities in Utah, there is a nonprofit called Encircle. Thanks to community donations, they renovated homes that are open after school for LGBTQ+ youth to hang out, obtain free mental health and gender therapy, and be involved with art and music programs. It is 100 percent free for the kids and parents who want to be empowered and utilize these resources.

I visited the Salt Lake City Encircle house in 2019 and met with some of the people whose lives it has enriched. The home is beautiful and some locations see more than sixty kids a day. Their mission is to offer chosen family and show our youth what a home can look and feel like. It is so cool that these Utah teens are able to have a space to grow and make friends with trained therapists and strong community leaders under the same roof! For more information go to encircletogether.org or reach out to your local LGBTQ+ center to see what's benefiting the community near you!

DATING

Queer storylines portrayed in TV shows and movies that I searched for in my teens continuously surrounded two main story arcs: coming out or falling in love. Both of these are sweet sentiments; but they didn't prepare me for my first queer heartbreaks. I remember, as my first relationship approached its end, wishing I had a parent I could run to for advice like I'd seen my heterosexual friends do when they needed support. **I wanted someone older to confide in whom I'd seen firsthand have a strong marriage or relationship.**

When coming out doesn't sit well with those around you, asking for relationship advice on the relationship they didn't support you having isn't really an option.

I was eventually able to seek the type of guidance I craved from a parent, once enough communication and time had resulted in a strengthened relationship. Maybe you aren't there yet with the people in your family, so if at any point you need relationship advice, refer back to this page!

Hello! Big brother Miles here with some advice on dealing with your first queer heartbreak. A lot of kids have their identities heavily intertwined with their relationships. **I've had many friends come out not by saying "I'm gay," but by saying, "I'm dating _____" or "I'm in love with _____."**

"I wanted someone older to confide in whom I'd seen firsthand have a strong marriage or relationship."

If that relationship comes to an end, that can leave a lot of room for feeling insecure, or maybe even questioning your identity, since a big part of why you came out is no longer there.

We are constantly growing with every person who enters our lives. The more points of view you encounter, the more your ideas are challenged, strengthened, or changed entirely. The end of a chapter with someone in your life doesn't mean the end of your story though! **The label you choose to define you only reflects YOU.** And you don't need to be with someone to feel valid in that label. I think queer breakups can also be so challenging because maybe there aren't a lot of out people that you know of in your area. There can be a fear that if it doesn't work out with one person, then you will surely be alone because who else is there? **You are going to meet so many people in your life!** I remember feeling so alone inside the bubble of my hometown thinking the only queer people were ones I knew on the Internet from communities hours and hours away. **Lean on friends and trusted people during this healing period and remember that life is always changing.**

"There can be a fear that if it doesn't work out with one person, then you will surely be alone because who else is there?"

1977: Harvey Milk became the first openly gay person to be elected to public office in the history of California. He won a seat on the San Francisco Board of Supervisors. He fought to end the legal discrimination against someone for their sexual orientation.

COMING OUT WITH YOUR GENDER IN SCHOOL

Many trans kids change their name and/or pronouns to affirm their identity. Some don't have access to do so legally, or their state won't allow it, so communicating your social transition to your school can be nerve racking if the name on the roster doesn't match what you go by.

At every school, coming out is different. Some kids go to a nonaccepting religious school, a school where everyone has known them their entire lives, a school where a family member works. Maybe you're the new kid or a class president. Coming out to people you know can be stressful and coming out to a student body can be even more so. Take a deep breath (and if you're in a binder, take two). The most important thing to remember is that you have a vibrant community to lean on and support you!

JOSEPHINE BAKER (1906–1975) was a successful singer and dancer. She grew up impoverished in Missouri and became one of the highest-paid performers in Europe during the 1920s! She was also bisexual and had a notable romance with another bisexual artist, Frida Kahlo. If you're bisexual, remember that badass bitches dancing and making famous art a hundred years ago were too!

TIP #1 **Find an ally.** Is there a teacher or faculty member who is an ally you feel comfortable coming out to? Even if you don't have their class, is there someone who works at the school who will support you?

TIP #2 **Explore support centers.** Are you familiar with an LGBTQ+ center near you? Many organizations have trans counselors who can offer support and help you communicate with your school.

TIP #3 **Communicate.** Start a group chain with the principal, all your teachers, and the faculty members you came out to, to help hold everyone accountable. Maybe add in your supportive parent/guardian or someone from the local LGBTQ+ center too!

TIP #4 **Send an email addressing your social transition to everyone!** Check out the next page for an example.

Template For a Coming-Out Email

Dear faculty,

My name is [PREFERRED NAME], and I attend your classes this semester. I will be in your roster as [BIRTH NAME]. I have recently come out as transgender, and I haven't legally changed my birth name/gender marker yet. I would appreciate it if I were referred to as [PREFERRED NAME] in your class and that [PREFERRED PRONOUNS] pronouns be used when referring to me. I have copied in [local LGBTQ+ center representative? A supportive family member?] so we can help answer any questions you may have. Thank you for the support, and I look forward to learning in your class!

Sincerely,
[PREFERRED NAME]

Encourage your school/ administration to check out the resources provided by GLSEN— Gay, Lesbian & Straight Education Network—to help create an inclusive and safe environment in your school. They have downloadable LGBTQ+-inclusive curriculum on their website for teachers to add to their lesson plans for grades K through 12. The resources range from story times with queer characters to information on historical events that will empower students who see themselves reflected in history. They also have information for students on how to start a GSA (gay-straight alliance/gender sexuality alliance) and offer resources to get the club involved with activities during the school year. **Go to GLSEN.org for more information and encourage your teachers to advocate for a safer space in school!**

Katja ♥ Mila

TIPS FOR WHAT TO SAY IF A LOVED ONE COMES OUT, FROM LGBTQ+ TEENS!

"I love you!"

"We love you no matter what."

"Thank you for trusting me enough to tell me!"

"I will work on adjusting to your new name/pronouns. I'm happy you know what will make you feel the most you!"

"Thank you for telling me. I'll do my best to use the correct pronouns/be respectful!"

"Do you want to talk more about it? We can get pizza!"

"I love you just the way you are."

"Awesome! I accept and support you."

"What does [insert your label] mean? I'm glad you wanted to share this with me, and I'd love to learn more!"

"OK, I support you! You can talk to me about this whenever you want."

"I hear you and I see you. Congrats on figuring out your identity."

"That's completely OK! Thanks for being comfortable enough to share this with me."

LGBTQ+ CENTERS

I feel like I'm constantly on repeat, answering my online viewers' questions, continuously shouting, "Go to your local LGBTQ+ center!" or "Look up the closest one to you!" or "They have so many resources!" But when you live in a more rural part of the country, that advice is easy to dismiss. Maybe you've never seen a center or you think the town you're in holds so much homophobia there couldn't possibly be any support. I wanted to do the work for you so you know you're supported! For many of us kids who come out and are met with negative responses, our dream is to run to the nearest coast and live in an accepting area. But you don't have to be in West Hollywood or Portland or Seattle or New York to be accepted! LGBTQ+ centers are nonprofits that provide children, adults, and elders information, legal assistance, mental health services, health services, support groups . . . the list goes on! Even if a center is far from you, a quick call or search on their website can give you information about what organizations are making a positive change in your town! Remember the Encircle houses in Utah? **Even if you feel completely alone, there are people who have felt the same and created groups to make your queer/trans experience a positive one!**

Here's a bunch of centers as of 2019 filled with teen groups, parent counseling, tons of activities, and information to get you started! Do you see a center near you?

"You don't have to be in West Hollywood or Portland or Seattle or New York to be accepted!"

Birmingham, Alabama—
Magic City Acceptance Center
MagicCityAcceptanceCenter.org

 Anchorage, Alaska—Identity, Alaska
IdentityAlaska.org

 Phoenix, Arizona—One N Ten
OneNTen.org

 Fayetteville, Arkansas—
NWA Center for Equality
NWAEquality.org

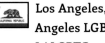 Los Angeles, California—Los
Angeles LGBT Center on Highland
LALGBTCenter.org

 Boulder, Colorado—Out Boulder
OutBoulder.org

 Norwalk, Connecticut—Triangle
Community Center
CTPrideCenter.org/youth

 Washington, District of Columbia—
The DC Center for the LGBT
Community
theDCCenter.org

 Miami, Florida—Pridelines Miami
Pridelines.org

 Savannah, Georgia—Savannah LGBT
Community Center
Firstcitynetwork.org

 Honolulu, Hawaii—Hawaii LGBT
Legacy Foundation
HawaiiLGBTLegacyFoundation.com

 Pocatella, Idaho—All Under One Roof
LGBT Centers of S.E.
AllUnderOneRoof.org

 Moline, Illinois—Quad Citians
Affirming Diversity
QCADOutforGood.org

 South Bend, Indiana—The LGBT
Center
TheLGBTQCenter.org

 West Des Moines, Iowa—One Iowa
OneIowa.org

 Louisville, Kentucky—Louisville
Youth Group, Inc.
LouisvilleYouthGroup.org

 Multiple locations, Maine—
Equality Maine
EqualityMaine.org/about-us

 Baltimore, Maryland—Pride Center
of Maryland
PrideCenterMD.org

Boston, Massachusetts—Boston Alliance of Gay, Lesbian, Bisexual & Transgender Youth (BAGLY)
BAGLY.org

 Detroit, Michigan—LGBT Detroit
LGBTDetroit.org

 Minnesota—Out Front Minnesota
OutFront.org

 Kansas City, Missouri—Kansas City Center for Inclusion
InclusiveKC.org

 Missoula, Montana—Western Montana Gay & Lesbian Community Center
GayMontana.org

 Lincoln, Nebraska—Outnebraska
OutLinc.org

 Las Vegas, Nevada—Gay and Lesbian Community Center of Southern Nevada
TheCenterLV.com

Portsmouth, New Hampshire—Seacoast Outright
SeaCoastOutright.org

 Highland Park, New Jersey—The Pride Center of New Jersey, Inc.
PrideCenter.org

 Albuquerque, New Mexico—Transgender Resource Center of New Mexico
Tgrcnm.org

 Brooklyn, New York—Brooklyn Community Pride Center
LGBTBrooklyn.org

 Asheville, North Carolina—Youth Outright, Inc.
YouthOutright.org

 Cleveland, Ohio—The LGBT Community Center of Greater Cleveland
LGBTCleveland.org

 Tulsa, Oklahoma—Dennis R. Neill Equality Center
OKEq.org

 Portland, Oregon—Q Center
PDXQCenter.org

 Philadelphia, Pennsylvania—The Attic Youth Center
AtticYouthCenter.org

Providence, Rhode Island—Youth Pride, Inc.
YouthPrideRI.org

 North Charleston, South Carolina—We Are Family
WeAreFamilyCharleston.org

 Sioux Falls, South Dakota—Sioux Falls Pride
SiouxFallsPride.org

 Memphis, Tennessee—Outmemphis:
The LGBTQ Center for the Mid-South
OutMemphis.org

San Antonio, Texas—The Center—Pride Center San Antonio
PrideCenterSA.org

 Salt Lake City, Utah—Utah Pride Center
UtahPrideCenter.org

 Burlington, Vermont—Pride Center of Vermont
PrideCenterVT.org

 Richmond, Virginia—Diversity Richmond
DiversityRichmond.org

 Seattle, Washington—Lambert House
LambertHouse.org

 Madison, Wisconsin—Outreach LGBT Community Center
OutreachMadisonLGBT.org

Multiple locations, Wyoming—Wyoming Equality
WyomingEquality.org

Fucking love you

MILES TO GO

MY TRANSITION AND HOW TO LIVE OUT AND PROUD

Transitioning can be thought of much like transportation: It's not how you get somewhere (by boat, plane, on foot, by car, etc.). It's the journey itself. **There is no checklist of changes you have to make in order to be trans—many people's transitions look different!** Some people want many physical changes and others want none. Not everyone has access to transgender healthcare; some can't undergo certain affirming changes due to medical or safety reasons; and for some, it just doesn't affirm them to transition using surgery or hormones. **My journey started with a name/pronoun change, then I went through hormone replacement therapy for some time, then top surgery.** I didn't make these decisions because I came out as trans. Rather, these were the steps I needed to take to feel and be seen as me.

An individual's transition is completely personal! I also just happened to be well known on (*throws glitter*) the Internet and very passionate about bringing LGBTQ+ issues and information to light on my channel. Although I am very open and choose to share my experiences, that also isn't a shared theme among all trans individuals. Or anyone in the community for that matter!

First and foremost, people transition so they can be seen as who they are (whatever that means to them). Their identity isn't automatically an invitation to ask personal or intrusive questions. We are so lucky to live in an age where we have access to the Internet and many people with a trans experience have shared their journeys! **If you or someone in your life has non-intrusive questions about the experience of transitioning, ask Google before you ask a stranger.**

"First and foremost, people transition so they can be seen as who they are (whatever that means to them). Their identity isn't automatically an invitation to ask personal or intrusive questions."

WAYS YOU CAN SUPPORT A TRANSGENDER/ NONBINARY PERSON

1 If you aren't asking for pronouns, ask the Internet or ask for permission to ask questions.

2 Listen to them! Every experience is different and may not be the same as another trans friend you have. Like me writing this book, one person isn't the expert on the community, they are an expert on their own journey.

3 If you mess up pronouns, quickly apologize, correct, and carry on with the conversation. "She said . . . excuse me, he said . . ." A long-winded apology in front of other people can be extremely uncomfortable and embarrassing. And acting like it didn't happen can add confusion for others and the person who was misgendered. Acknowledge your mistake, correct it, continue the conversation, and work on making the switch.

4 If you are going to buy trans-related merchandise, buy from a transgender person. Put your money toward that community and an organization that supports it! Same goes for queer art/media! Look at where your money is going when you are trying to be an ally for a certain identity.

As you already know, I started my social transition by first changing my name. But unlike most other trans people, I transitioned in front of millions of people who watched me become the Miles that I am today.

My first coming-out for my gender identity—I don't think many new people know this—was for being nonbinary. **To me, nonbinary meant being free from all gender expectations.** My entire life I was asked, "Are you a boy or are you a girl?" First it came from kids on the playground as I hid my long hair under beanies. And later (once I lived on my own, free from expectations and biases), the question came from myself. I honestly was so burnt out on this whole gender thing!

Coming out as nonbinary was me giving myself the freedom to do whatever I felt was unique to me, without the pressure of masculine/feminine labels. From that freedom, I started to graduate into myself—first with the help of a social transition (my name/pronouns), and later a medical transition (with hormones, to masculinize my body). Over time, as I slowly started to be read as male, I found that it fit. Your labels may change, and that's OK. I'm thankful for the freedom and community around me that have helped me define myself.

It took a while to get to this place of freedom and contentment, though. I had a really slow transition. **It took a long**

time for people to not misgender me. It was really rough because in my day-to-day life, people were misgendering me in public and then in my safe space on the Internet, people who had been watching my videos had stopped for a while because I hadn't been posting, and when they came back, they were using my dead name because they had missed that one video where I came out. Coming out to a large online platform had its ups and downs! In part due to hormonal side effects like cystic acne and anxiety, I took multiple breaks from sharing online to focus on my mental health. **Taking breaks from social media around this time was a way for me to show myself kindness during my transition.**

I think a big misconception with transitioning is that it happens overnight. From doctor appointments to legal dates, pronoun mistakes, and hormonal changes, transitioning was a process! I owe a huge thanks to all the like-minded humans who saw me as me. Having a community online as well as off was so important for my growth, and I hope the spaces I've created online can be that community for someone else.

Rewritten clearer :

2018 ✓

☀ Hey ☀ I'm **MILES** AND I'M

OUT of the closet, the lives of unsupportive people and excuses not to be ‑ME‑.

ADD? I went through my journals from the year I came out and found a suicide letter from every month.

Around that time I used to hated the cheesy phrase "IT GETS BETTER" Like... lol okay...when? Like can we get the dates it got bad for everyone and compare it to when all their problems magically went away? Can we average those numbers for me? Is it 6 months? 6 years? When? Also where are these happy people because I don't know them.

VERS ↑ STAR

Tweet   ▫ ▬ ▢
MILES
9:54 AM 3/4/17

It took 2 years 2 months and 2 days ~~~~~ and a lot of character development for it to get better.
alt word?

If I could go back in time to my half in half out of the closet self I would have no advice to give. I don't think there's any outside words that can magicly solve a problem. And knowing my stubborn ass I definitly wouldn't of taken it.

WHAT is it with knowing that makes gender so instinct to us? Because I'm not into "masculine" things and having a "masculine" form because I was told this is what a boy looks like. It's just always been me. I've always wanted blue, and a skateboard and action figures and to fuck. It's just funny how we are coded that way.

I AM A BOY
    I ALWAYS HAVE BEEN.
I AWAIT THE DAYS
THAT ISN'T QUESTIONED

2018

HOW DO YOU SEE ME?
WHAT DO YOU SEE?
WHAT IS FEMININE ABOUT
ME? WHAT DO YOU SEE?
DO YOU SEE A MOTHER?
COULD YOU SEE ME BEING
A CHILD? WHAT DO YOU
SEE? WHY DO YOU CALL
ME HE? BECAUSE I TOLD
YOU TO? OR BECAUSE I
JUST AM AND I BARE THE
BURDEN OF HAVING TO
ALTER MY FORM. AND
IM CONFUSED WHY I DO
IT?

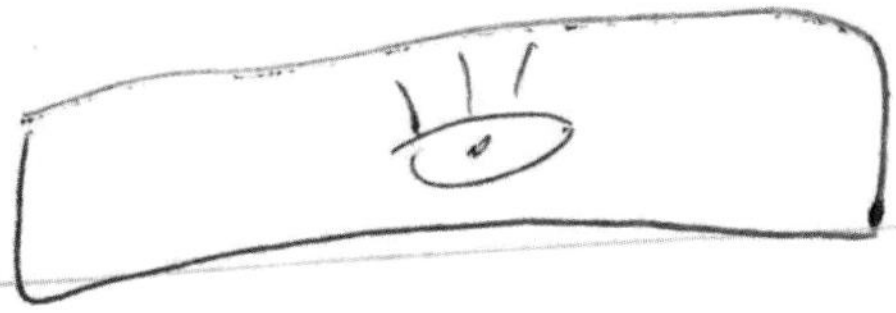

I HAVE A COOL NAME

I THINK IM BETTER
AT HELPING OTHERS THAN
MYSELF. I THINK IM GOOD
AT SHOWING LOVE AND
KINDNESS TOWARDS OTHERS.

I THINK I'LL TAKE
SOME NIGHTS TO GO
TAG IN STRANGE
PARTS OF TOWN AND
WALK AND LISTEN
TO MUSIC.

I AGGRESSIVELY WANT TO
LIVE AND FEEL LIKE ME.

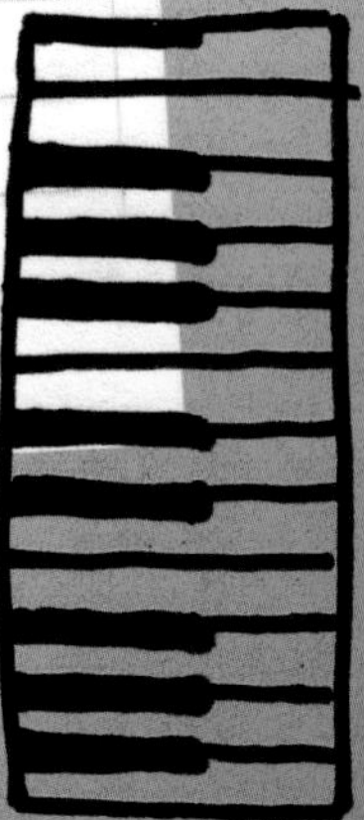

2018

me bitching about bullshit.

HOPE NO ONE ELSE READS THIS

I AM A GUY I AM A GUY

I KEEP TRYING TO IGNORE HOW SAD I AM.

I HOPE I AM NOT TOO SAD FOR THE PEOPLE I CARE ABOUT.

I WANT TO BE SEEN AS ME.

IT'S SO HARD TO RUN AWAY FROM THE PAST. IT SHOWS UP EVERYWHERE.

IN MY DREAMS I KEEP HIDING FROM PEOPLE. OR I'M UNDER WATER IN A SUBMARINE OR I'M IN SPACE.

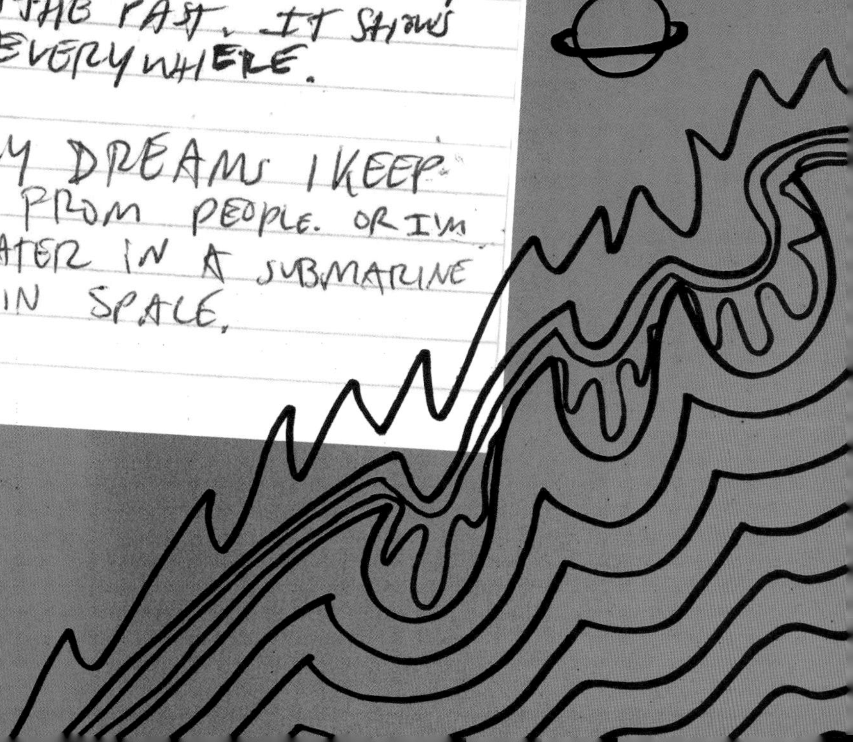

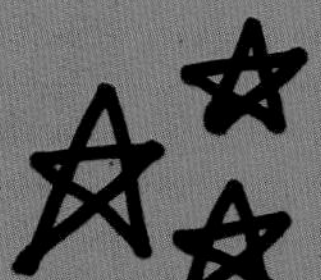

THING IS I HAVE NO PROBLEM
BEING SEEN BUT WHEN ITS
NOT ME THATS BEING Seen.
I CANT TAKE IT LIKE I
USED TO.

I HOPE I'M STRONG ENOUGH
FOR THE PEOPLE I keep
AROUND ME. I wanna
PUT THIS ANGER AND
FRUSTRATION AND SADNESS
AND DOUBT AND VULNRABILITY
INTO Something. BUT
WHAT I HAVE BEEN DEDICATING
MYSELF TO MY WHOLE LIFE
BRINGS ME BACK INTO
THAT CYCLE IT DOESNT
FREE ME FROM IT.

2018

HOW TO DISCOVER YOUR GENDER EXPRESSION

Let's talk about some clear and easy ways you can approach your transition.

"I DON'T LIKE THE WAY I FEEL IN MY CLOTHES"

Would dressing in a more traditionally masculine or feminine way make you feel more comfortable? For me, the word "fashion" used to represent the pink, frilly, and lacy chains that confined me to the body of a person everyone thought I was. It was synonymous with tight bra straps, scoop-neck shirts, and tote bags to carry my books to school. Growing up, if I knew I wanted a blue shirt and black pants, leave it to fashion and the "girls' section" to make me see a stranger when I looked in the mirror. I consistently felt out of place wearing clothes that were picked out for my gender marker.

And when I wore clothes that did fit more than just my body, I didn't fit everyone's small minds, even though I felt better. Please take my advice from years of mastering the art of not giving a f**k: No matter what you do, you will never please everyone! You might as well be yourself and let like-minded people follow you on your path of living an authentic life!

After I came out as queer, something clicked in me. I learned I didn't need to dress for anyone but myself. (Thankfully I was in an environment where I could do so safely.) While I was going through significant character development in the months following my coming-out, I started finding my gender expression. The most significant discovery I had was thanks to outrageous Instagram baddies wearing platform boots and rainbow hoodies. I would continuously scroll through dozens of profiles featuring people wearing unexpected styles, a lot of which generated hundreds of thousands of likes.

Seeing other people as outwardly self-confident gave me the silent OK to express my own fashion identity with confidence. This is also something I hope to pass along to people who find me online. I began to realize that "cute" doesn't exist. At least not in the way it had been taught to me by the generation before mine, with a narrow concept of gender expression, the kind that only celebrates beauty pageant girls in magazines. **"Ugly" and "beautiful" are both subjective terms, but confidence reaches all eyes.** As long as you love something and you own it—your love for it and the way you present yourself—that's what makes you attractive! It sounds corny, I know, but it's true! Once you allow yourself to believe it—and I mean fully buy into the idea that everything is ugly and beautiful at the same time—your world opens up, and you stop comparing yourself to people you don't want to be.

"No matter what you do, you will never please everyone!"

AWAITING JANUARY 2018

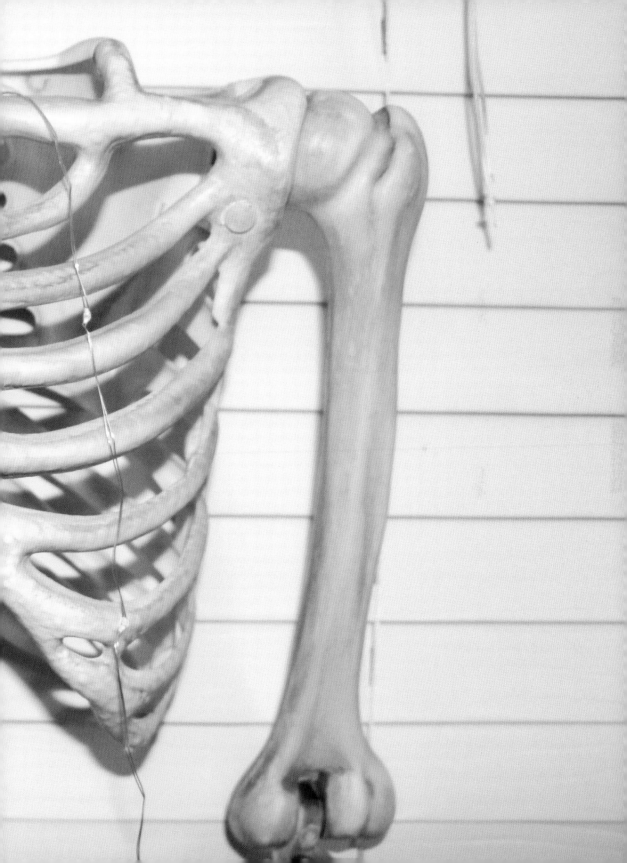

Though I was finally feeling comfortable in my clothes, I later realized there was something I still needed to get off my chest . . . it was my chest (*slaps knee*). When my first binder arrived after I ordered it online, I felt an instant connection, and I tried on every shirt I owned to see how I looked. (And this was even before I allowed myself to reach the—at the time—daunting and obvious conclusion that I'm a guy, as binders aren't used exclusively by transmasculine folks.) Binding, much like my haircut (which I'll talk about later), was a serendipitous discovery that could make me feel more confident and comfortable than I had ever imagined—and not exclusive to any specific label.

Many affirming articles of clothing or medical interventions can be costly and not accessible to all members of the community. A nonprofit based in Oregon that I love is Point of Pride. They distribute donated binders/femme shapewears and provide financial assistance for top surgery/electrolysis. Packages are discreet and they are here if you need support! For more information on how to apply and what they offer, go to PointofPride.org.

(Traditionally) Masculine Shopping Tips:

#1   **Short-sleeved button-downs!** They are easy to find in fun patterns, both casual and crazy. This style accentuates the broadness of your shoulders and hides the chest region.

#2   **Binding!** My favorite binder brand was GC2B. They have a wide variety of skin tones and sizes ranging from XXS to 5XL as of 2019. They also have ample information on finding your perfect size, as well as safety tips! You should never bind with ACE bandages or with other unsafe methods. GC2B is a product that is "designed by trans people for trans people that is safe, accessible, and comfortable." For more information, check out GC2B.com.

#3   **Color!** When shopping with traditionally masculine styles in mind, it can be hard to find colorful items. When I was first shopping for myself after my transition, it was hard for me to find anything that wasn't dark-toned and also worked for my body. I didn't want to be seen as feminine and therefore didn't want attention drawn to my chest. Fashion stopped seeming limitless and started having "rules" once my dysphoria kicked in. My tip, if you're feeling this way, is to integrate color with your pants. A black shirt that camouflages your chest can go with any pattern and color pant. It will allow you to have fun with your wardrobe without stressing over your physique.

"I HATE/LOVE/ DON'T KNOW HOW TO WEAR MAKEUP"

Embrace, reject, or repurpose makeup to suit how you want to look. Before I discovered my gender expression, I felt compelled to wear makeup because I thought it was what I was supposed to do. No matter how you identify, makeup is for anyone who wants to wear it! I traded in my eyeliner and foundation for Glossier's boy brow pencil to darken and thicken my brows, giving them a more masculine, unkempt look. And I said goodbye to feeling like I needed to do anything that wasn't aligned with me being me. **Fashion and makeup don't need to be all girl or all boy.** It's whatever energy you're inspired by and whatever makes you feel like yourself. It's up to you to discover what that looks like.

141

"I DON'T LIKE THE WAY I LOOK WITH MY HAIR"

What are the steps you need to take to change your style? Will you need to talk to a parent first? Can you start by pushing your hair into beanies or buying a wig or extensions? Cutting my hair short was a constant internal battle with myself and external battle with family members that lasted as long as most haircut appointments I can remember. The reason why I wanted it short wasn't clear to me for the longest time when I was a kid. I just didn't have the language to know I was a boy or that I was trans. **My earliest memories are of me just knowing I would feel more like me with a shorter cut— it was as simple as that.**

Unfortunately, I didn't end up getting it cut the way I wanted until I was nineteen, and I spent years with a crooked bob as a compromise with my parents. That was as short as they were willing to let it go! There were also plenty of years of having long, unruly hair scratching my face as I tried to conform to social norms. I'd shove it into beanies and slick it back into a ponytail to cope. It was super confusing navigating my personal style as a teenager while also caring about what other people thought (because I was a teenager). I was constantly complimented on how my hair looked "so pretty," which made my desire to cut my hair even more confusing for a teen who really wanted to feel good and fit in. What if I was making a mistake? A part of me acknowledges today that it is

144

> ## "It's as if I looked in the mirror and actually saw myself for the first time."

just hair and it's ridiculous that so many people have opinions on how someone else looks. If anything, it's the one area that should be the easiest for us to play with, but straying from what everyone else in your community is doing or saying can be hard.

When I ended up getting "the big haircut," it was surprisingly emotional. **(Shout-out to everyone who told me not to—you were wrong.)** It's as if I looked in the mirror and actually saw myself for the first time. Now, maybe you've never felt this, and you naturally feel alignment with the way you are on the outside and the way you feel on the inside.

But for teenage Miles, it took years to reach gender euphoria after a trip to the barber. That appointment was, unbeknownst to me, a relief from my gender dysphoria before I even knew what that was. I think it's important to point out that not all AFAB (assigned female at birth) people who want their hair cut short at a young age are trans—I just happened to be. Gender expressions and gender identities can be mixed and matched in many ways. Maybe changing your hair will make you feel more like you!

STORMÉ DELARVERIE (1920–2014) was known as the "lesbian Rosa Parks" and one of the leaders of the Stonewall rebellion. The Stonewall Inn is a popular gay and drag bar in New York and was the site of one of the most influential LGBTQ+ riots in history. The effects of that event aided in the formation of many modern-day organizations, activism, and even pride parades.

Stormé was a butch lesbian drag king who fought against police who were unjustifiably arresting people that night on account of them being LGBTQ+. Being queer and cross-dressing used to be criminalized in America. And due to sodomy laws, homosexuality in parts of the country was still criminalized up until 2003!

Queer, trans women of color and drag queens famously fought for freedom and our rights at the Stonewall rebellion. You may have heard of some of these faces of the rebellion: Marsha "Pay it no mind" Johnson (1945–1992) and Sylvia Rivera (1951–2002).

Have you ever been to a pride parade? There's a lot of celebration with festivals, marches, music, and proud people. You may have heard unsupportive people say things about them like, "Why isn't there a straight pride?" or "Why do gay people have to rub it in everyone's face that they're gay?" The first pride events weren't born out of celebration but out of a fight to gain fundamental rights and freedoms that have historically been denied to LGBTQ+ people. Pride parades are a reminder of the prejudice that is out there and the strength in all of us. If someone questions why they don't have a straight parade, they should be thankful that they don't need one. And if someone tries to silence you for celebrating your queerness, remember those people who identified just like you who yelled louder.

Guide

to a Masculine Haircut

No matter what style your first chop is, it'll be epic! In my opinion, this first cut isn't so much about looks as it is about taking control of how you present yourself. **Your personal touch and how you style your hair and preferences on the cut will come after some time of having it. Looking back, my first short haircut was still way too long for my taste and much too feminine looking. But, at the time, I didn't realize that. My confidence went higher due to the ten inches they cut off and that was all I was focused on. Worst-case scenario: It's a bad haircut. But a bad haircut will always grow out, and you'll know more about what you do and don't want!** My advice is to always bring in a picture of the type of cut you want. **Maybe an old style from Ruby Rose or a newer fade from a random person you follow online. Here's a little guide to some cuts you may want to try to complement your facial structure/vibe.**

Androgynous/masculine cuts

COMB-OVER SIDE PART SLICKED TO THE SIDE: If you're willing to spend time putting product in your new hair, this look is all face and all business.

CURLY FRINGE CUT: You never really know how your hair will lay when you get it cut short for the first time. My hair was super curly when it was long but then very wavy when short. If you think you have the curly gene, this is super fairy boy realness!

CLASSIC POMPADOUR: Retro!

SLICKED-BACK QUIFF WITH SHAVED SIDES: Very badass, especially for the first cut.

FADED CREW CUT:
This one will grow out nicely.

THE FAUXHAWK:
I mean, come on, this is what we dream about doing with our short hair!

SPIKEY WINDSWEPT FRINGE:
My haircut when I add product to tame my curls!

MOHAWK: The power move I wish I'd chosen for my first short haircut!

BUZZED SIDES WITH A LONG-LAYERED COMB-OVER: Super punk and very masculine!

PIXIE CUT: So sweet! More on the androgynous spectrum.

SIDE-SWEPT SHAVED CUT: Very edgy.

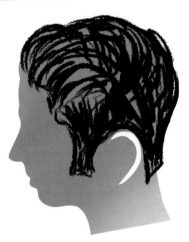

SIDEBURNS: Most feminine short cuts will trim the sideburns at an angle while masculine cuts are squared off. Before I passed as a male, I would always tell my barber to square my sides; it really makes a huge difference!

"WHAT ABOUT MY OTHER BODY HAIR?"

Growing up AFAB, I never understood why girls had to shave their legs and armpits and boys didn't. I could tell a tale of how I was breaking gender stereotypes since I was in elementary school by refusing to shave my legs and sticking up for my freedom to groom how I please. Even in the face of adversity, I scoffed at razors and was content with my body's evolutionary need to wick away sweat and regulate my temperature with hair. Down with the patriarchy! Up with follicles! OK, so maybe that's not the whole truth.

First and foremost, I was a lazy preteen and was not happy when I was told to go to the bathroom and shave twice a week. (Yes, I was told to shave, by peers and family members.) But that desire that was pushed on me by women who were too insecure to wear shorts on a hot day, because of stubble and various soap advertisements with catchy jingles, didn't make sense to me. **It was literally just hair. What did it matter what I did with it?** Especially if half of the population isn't required to shave?

"First and foremost, I was a lazy preteen and was not happy when I was told to go to the bathroom and shave twice a week."

This frustration never left me. It led me to create the most important video I have ever made in my life (drum roll please): **"DYEING MY LEG HAIR PURPLE."** In the video, I literally did just that, but I also talk about my distrust in anyone who says that someone has to do something with their body just because of their gender. All the while, I was lathering purple dye below my thighs and turning my shins a nice shade of lavender that would last a month. I say that was the most important video because it was seen by millions of people.

Walking around with purple leg hair sparked some negative comments in my personal life, but online, hundreds of thousands of kids felt the same way I did. And thus, a community was formed, and validation was gained! **Your body is just that—yours!** Play with your presentation by changing up your grooming routine and see how you feel. Although I'd sometimes get looks from strangers who clearly thought my body hair was gross and unsightly (gasp!), it felt more natural to me than shaving just because I was told to. Challenge your daily routine and ask yourself afterward if you're doing it because you like the way you look or because it's what's expected of you.

June 26, 2015: Same-sex marriage was legalized in all fifty states of America! January of that year is when I came out with my sexuality. I got "the haircut" that same month!

"Challenge your daily routine and ask yourself afterward if you're doing it because you like the way you look or because it's what's expected of you."

"I THINK I WANT TO CHANGE MY NAME/ PRONOUNS"

How exciting! Changing my name was one of the best decisions I have ever made but also one of the scariest. I had built it up in my head for years until I made the switch with the support from my great, queer chosen family! People online often ask how I picked a name that was right for me. I imagine people think I always had this name in mind and once that one syllable rolled off my tongue [mahylz], I knew it would follow me forever. *poof* *sparkle* *sparkle* *sparkle* It actually wasn't that dramatic, but the change was still essential.

I had no idea what name I wanted to be called for the rest of my life. That was way too stressful. **What I did know for sure was that I did not want the name I was given at birth.** My birth name was incredibly feminine, and on a basic level, it inhibited people from seeing me as me. The fear of people not accepting my new name or not picking the "right" name made that leap very scary. Which is totally valid; this was new territory, and I wasn't sure how to ask for support from the people I trusted. **Even though I didn't know what I would change my name to, I knew for sure my name needed to be more masculine.** I was willing to accept that truth and pick a name since there was a higher chance of me feeling more comfortable and confident with it instead of staying stagnant with my old one.

You may not always know precisely what you want, but you can use your knowledge of what you don't want to get you there. I went back and forth on whether I should change my name for years, considering many names in the process. After opening up to my chosen family of queer friends

Renaming Tips:

 Have a few close friends start referring to you in whatever way you see fit; you don't have to announce it to everyone or make any legal switch yet.

 Allow yourself to be honest about your feelings toward the jumble of sounds people use to refer to you and move forward with that.

 Not all trans people rename themselves and not all people who rename themselves are trans!

 If you're not sure if you want more femininity or masculinity in your name, try ordering takeout with some friends and give the restaurant your potential preferred name! Wait in a group as you hear the employee call it and make eye contact with you. See how you feel! I made many coffee shop trips with my crew during my first month as Miles.

about my inner battle, they gave me the support I needed to make the first step. We sifted through hundreds of baby boy names; sometimes I said them aloud in the mirror, sometimes I wrote them down. **Eventually, I picked a name and kept it just between me and my friends until I knew it felt right to me.**

When I changed my name, it just stuck. I felt so much more confident introducing myself to new people and started telling more and more friends about the switch. At this point in my timeline, I was just beginning to come out as transgender. I wasn't sure where I fell on the spectrum—nonbinary or FTM (female to male, damn you, labels and uncertainty)—but I did know I needed the name change for me to be my most authentic self.

NAMES I CONSIDERED:

KADE

ADAM

EVAN

MAX

RIVER

JOSH

ALEX

RILEY

REESE

JAMIE

MICHAEL DILLON

(1915–1962) was a British transgender man and naval surgeon. He's known for publishing one of the first memoirs documenting the journey of a trans man as well as being one of the first to successfully undergo bottom surgery as part of his medical transition. Many people learned about transitioning through his visibility. However, the constant bombardment from the media led him to flee to India, where he lived out the rest of his life as a monk. Your mental health should always take priority. Listen to your body!

FINDING AND SEEING A GENDER THERAPIST

A gender therapist is a licensed therapist who specializes in talking to people about their gender identity, expression, dysphoria, euphoria—basically, all things gender! They are also equipped to write you letters to start medically transitioning, which, in some cases, is required depending on your age, region, healthcare, doctor, etc. I started seeing my gender therapist when I began questioning my gender identity to get clarity on what it was that I was feeling. Talking to a specialist who was knowledgeable in the area of gender, and being open and honest about how I was feeling played a significant role in my having the strength to come out. It was also a super validating experience.

I remember being anxious about seeing a therapist because I thought that meant I was solidifying my transgender identity when that wasn't the case. **Gender therapy is really for anyone who feels like they have something "going on" with their gender.** You may not have the language to express how you're feeling, so speaking

"Talking to a specialist and being open and honest about how I was feeling played a significant role in my having the strength to come out."

Finding a gender therapist can be tricky depending on where you live, but there are so many options out there. **You can rely on your community and ask trans people you know who they see.** Luckily, we live in the age of technology, so even if the only trans person you know is through the Internet, lots of gender therapists do their work over email, phone, and video calls. You can also call your local LGBTQ+ center to see what they offer and ask what they recommend near you. If you are a minor, asking your parent or guardian to take you to a gender therapist can be just as scary as coming out, but involving them in the process could be beneficial! Some therapists also offer family sessions to keep everyone educated and in the loop. This is the space to have conversations about potentially wanting to medically transition and ask whatever questions you may have. A gender therapist can also help with social transition questions like dating and coming out at school. There are many resources out there for you to feel supported in your search of what feels right and what is next!

An online therapy resource I know of is PrideCounseling.com. After filling out a questionnaire about your identity and recent mental health, you will be paired with a counselor who you can message or video chat with. It is super easy to audition multiple therapists until you find one who fits. The "message only" feature

with someone who has the vocabulary will help you gain that knowledge. Some people start gender therapy and find they don't need to transition, while others feel a strong need to transition after they have all information on how to affirm themselves. While talking to friends online and offline about your identity is helpful and validating, talking to a specialist is a highly recommended tool on your journey, especially if you are considering medically transitioning.

"Some people start gender therapy and find they don't need to transition, while others feel a strong need to transition after they have all information on how to affirm themselves."

is also great if you're nervous about a face-to-face session. This option does require payment! Check out Pride Counseling online and see if it's a good fit for you.

As for my own therapist, I first took a recommendation from a friend who was going through a social transition. **It turned out that this therapist, who was great for my friend, wasn't the right one for me.** I felt uncomfortable—the therapist was quiet and stoic, and I had no idea how to drive the conversation. I felt like the topics we talked about weren't helping me progress in any way. The thing is, you're not always going to find the right person right away. If anything, I learned what kind of therapist I did need, so I now knew what traits I was looking for to better support my needs. **Don't let one bad therapy session turn you off.** There's often a trial period when you see more than one therapist before you find the right one.

If you aren't using an app or online service that helps fit you with the right type of person immediately, you'll need to

do what I did: Get the names of therapists from your community, insurance, online forums, or from your local LGBTQ+ center (call or email for a consultation). You can consult with therapists in person or over the phone, usually for free, to see if they are the right fit. **If you don't know what you're looking for, then do what I did and go to a session or two and see what you gained or what you wish you'd gotten out of the experience.**

Opening up about my goals during my transition to a stranger was difficult at first. I eventually found a gender therapist who was also transgender, which made me feel a lot more comfortable, and I was able to grow a lot as a person. If I had attended gender therapy as a teenager, I would've felt so supported and fulfilled way sooner than I actually did. Therapy, gender-related or not, gives us tools to work through emotional baggage and release traumas. **The big takeaway is: Whether or not you start hormones or get surgery, support during your transition is important for any trans/gender-variant person.**

"Whether or not you start hormones or get surgery, support during your transition is important for any trans/gender-variant person."

I AM MILES

WHERE I AM NOW,
WHAT I HAVE LEARNED,
AND WHERE I'M GOING

We are so trained by the media (TV, books, movies, etc.) to consume stories where there is a clear beginning, clear ending, as well as a clear protagonist and a clear antagonist—but life isn't like that. **Life goes on after that coming-out moment and things are always changing.** Even with the publication of this book, my relationships will continue to grow stronger, or they could move in another direction.

So what are the relationships with my family like now? I'm apprehensive about writing this for many anxiety-fueled reasons. Nonetheless, I think it's important for that kid who has only seen one type of happy coming-out ending to see mine. I got that coming-out, happy ending I always wanted, because I feel 100 percent happy with who I am and with the people who support me. I have some family members who I am now so close to, some who didn't

> **"The good relationships I have didn't all happen overnight. They entailed constant effort from both sides."**

even take my initial coming-out well. And I have other family members who I had to distance myself from in order to live my truth. Not to mention my chosen family, who has had my back along the way!

The good relationships I have didn't all happen overnight. They entailed constant effort from both sides with the overarching theme that we wanted to have a relationship. And some took years and resources like educational

LGBTQ+ blogs and videos from other parents of queer youth to nurture those relationships until they fully blossomed. **It's not like we had a big movie moment conversation in the rain with tears and apologies and a big rainbow appeared in the sky.** It was an accumulation of little texts that said "I love you," and random calls midday to say that they had heard about what I was doing and they were proud of me.

If there's a lesson here for a parent to keep a relationship with their child, it's just as simple as that. Just love your kid. Vulnerability and accountability can be mighty mountains to climb, but the burden can be shared. *Just love your kid.* **The advice I can give to the child in this situation is it's OK to let people in.** At times, I found myself wishing I had a relationship with certain people; but I was holding on to so much anger and resentment from the past that I wouldn't pick up the phone for them when they called.

Relationships, especially ones after emotional trauma, are hard work. I started to answer their phone calls. I created and conveyed boundaries that I set for myself to have a healthy relationship: **"My name is Miles, and my pronouns are he/him. If you can't say that right now that's fine, but then please don't call me anything—I will not respond."** So yes, our relationship isn't the same; it's better because it's real. With coming into your own and coming out, the best love you are going to receive is a love that's intended for you. If I wore a mask for the rest of my life and was unfulfilled for the sake of keeping relationships afloat, then the phone calls I'd receive wouldn't truly be meant for me. I'm now able to look in the mirror and love who I am, hold the hand of someone I love, and still hear that phone ringing.

I feel the same amount of gratitude for the unhealthy relationships I became strong enough to discontinue when boundaries couldn't be met. Some relationships are toxic and unhealthy to continue. **If you are living under the same roof as your parents, it's OK to guard parts of your identity out of safety and preservation of your mental health.** If you are living on your own, it's OK not to have relationships with family members for the same reason. And conversely, it's a two-way street to have a good and healthy relationship. **It is OK to forgive and teach the ones you love who are willing to learn.** Relationships continuously evolve and change.

The most important thing is your safety, and there are support systems in place to help those who need it. Many LGBTQ+ centers offer therapy for parents and children, as well as communities that bring parents of queer youth together to serve as support for each other.

SOME OTHER THINGS I'VE LEARNED:

HOW TO GET THROUGH A PANIC ATTACK

With any change, there's a chance of anxiety. Even though I'm in a good place in my life, my anxiety is something that can always creep up on me. But now I have the tools to fight back. The following tips have worked for me, but of course I'm not a doctor, and everyone's different. If you ever feel like you're in physical danger, call your doctor!

In an anxiety attack, the first thing you need to know is this: You are going to be OK. The first time I felt real panic was during my first coming-out. I blacked out most of the interaction and was motionless. It took hundreds of panic attacks before I was able to identify triggers that set them off and gather information on what calms me down when it happens.

Here are a few tips that may help you!

Listen to your body! Do you need to be alone or do you need to be around like-minded people? I've been in different anxious states where I've required space, or I've needed lots of community. Listen to your body; it is OK to leave an event or group to take a moment for yourself. When I feel a panic attack coming on in public, I will excuse myself to go to the restroom and take five minutes to be alone and assess what I need.

Write down everything you feel. Sometimes anxiety comes from a buildup of words that have gone unsaid for too long. Maybe the reason is that it stems from you having to hide part of yourself from someone close to you. Perhaps it's not as easy to define. Go ahead and word vomit in the notes of your phone or a journal meant only for you. Writing and getting it out can calm you down.

Repeat positive affirmations to yourself. "I am OK." "I am loved." "This feeling will pass." Speak comforting words to ground yourself in a positive state.

Try a grounding exercise to calm yourself. List five things you can physically see, four things you can touch, three things you can hear, two things you can smell, and one thing you can taste. Sometimes a state of panic can make our minds race and detach us from what is actually going on in the moment and this can help you focus on reality.

Focus on your breathing! Take a deep breath in with your nose, hold it for five seconds, and then exhale slowly through your mouth while relaxing all your muscles. Think about every part of your body and relax each part one by one as you continue to breathe in this rhythm.

Distract yourself! I've found that editing pictures in my phone during a long, anxiety-filled car ride—or painting when I'm teeming with anxiety at home—has really helped my panic subside! Watch a funny YouTube video! Try out a bunch of solo activities that you love, to see what helps you take your mind off of . . . your mind.

(Trigger Warning)

Before you read any further, if you ever feel alone or in danger of self-harm, the Trevor Project has a confidential crisis and suicide prevention lifeline that you can call 24-7 at 1-866-488-7386. If you don't feel comfortable talking on the phone, they also offer confidential support from professionals via text with TrevorText. This is also 24-7: Text "START" to 678678. Standard text messaging rates apply. And if texting isn't a safe option for you, TrevorChat is on their website, where you can instant message a crisis counselor. Visit TheTrevorProject.org/help to talk about your identity, or your coming out, or maybe something that hurt your feelings that day. You are not alone. People are here to listen and help!

LEARNING FROM SELF-HARM STORIES AND MY OWN EXPERIENCES

I was on my first American tour meeting hundreds of queer teens every weekend. Meet and greets are always high energy and intense, especially with an LGBTQ+ audience. A lot of kids, like myself, don't just watch a queer YouTuber because they're #goals (I'm sorry, I had to), but because they mirror their own identity in some way or the identity they aren't allowed to perform at home. I never used to be able to do a meet and greet without crying. **(Not now though, I'm very big and strong. *sniffles*)** On this 2017 tour, I started hearing self-harm survivor stories from my teenage audience.

I still have the bracelets and beanies given to me by survivors who opened up to me. If it weren't for those kids being vocal about their experiences, I wouldn't have had the strength to share mine as well. Even though I was energetic and carefree online when I was a teenager, when I was alone, I started to self-harm. It was a brief, dark period that my teenage self, along with countless others, had to do battle with every day. I felt defeated most of the time.

The night that it all changed, I was in my bathroom, the shower was on, music was playing, and I was crying on the floor. The typical thoughts were rushing through my head: "If only this. If only that." At this time in my adolescence I based my happiness around the way other people saw me and treated me. **I realized I was torturing myself with the same words that people were using against me.** While people in my town would (apparently) use religion as a reason to belittle me, I was using their

"At this time in my adolescence I based my happiness around the way other people saw me and treated me."

ignorance as a reason to belittle myself. Negativity from other people had become a justification for hurting myself.

Someone's words can influence another's actions, but words can't *create* actions. I realized I had all the power to get the life I wanted with the tools I had around me. Things could be better; and I could wallow in it, or I could be the best me with what I had and use it to ignite change. So that night I wrote out exactly what I wanted, who I wanted to be, and what I wanted to be doing a year from then. **Journaling was and still is a great tool for becoming self-aware and for reflecting.**

Massachusetts was the first U.S. state to legalize same-sex marriage on May 17, 2004! As well as the sixth jurisdiction in the world!

I started strengthening my relationships with people who identified similarly to me and cultivating my chosen family and offering education as defense to hate. I clung to the Internet and shared my humor and thoughts, and utilized that outlet creatively to let out frustrations. **With every positive comment and like, there was validation.** I started putting more stock in what I did have instead of in what I didn't, and this new perspective grew into a strong sense of self and clear vision for a bright future. **If you are battling with pulling yourself out of a dark time: I see you and I was you.** Processing negativity is something that isn't often taught to us in our youth. You are worth fighting for.

HOW TO LET GO OF INGRAINED NEGATIVITY

"Do things in love." I vaguely remember hearing about the Westboro Baptist Church when I was a teenager. It was started by a southern family who had created a campaign called "God Hates Fags." (I know, TEA.) If you're familiar with my videos, then you know I found this hilarious. Heartbreaking but hilarious. I've been known to prank call their home, asking for Jesus, as well as change my number to all sixes and claiming to be the savior. **(I am a very respectful and responsible human being, please be my friend.)**

Though I used their hatred for good comedic content, the visibility they brought to homophobia never sat well with me. I never would've guessed I would end up meeting one of the sons of the man who started the WBC and learning a few things about love. **This sounds like I'm about to tell a gay love story between me and a Westboro Baptist Church member.** Unfortunately, no. However, it is heartfelt and ties into our theme of coming out and it not going well.

"Do things in love."

There I was, a big gay meme, getting tacos with Nate Phelps, son of Fred Phelps, the late founder of the WBC. Nate left the church, and his family, on the night of his eighteenth birthday. As it was told to me, he'd packed a car that he had bought in secret that was parked a few blocks down from his house. As if in a fairy tale, the clock struck midnight as he left.

When I met him, it was decades later. He was an LGBTQ+ rights activist with a wife and children of his own. We spent an afternoon together filming a video in West Hollywood, the queer mecca of Los Angeles. Truly iconic. **Nate was adult-size proof that it is OK not to vocalize your beliefs if you are not in a safe environment.** And, it is OK not to have a relationship with blood relatives or anyone abusive. At the time, I was newly on my own and moving through a lot of emotions related to my strained-to-nonexistent relationships with family members.

Like most stubborn teens, I felt like I had learned everything I needed to take care of myself. But what I took away from my afternoon with Nate was about unlearning. He warned that years after leaving his abusive family's home, he would catch himself saying words that mirrored his father's, despite knowing his truth and choosing to leave behind his family's prejudiced attitudes. You can carry negativity with you from a negative

NANCY CÁRDENAS (1934–1994) was the first lesbian to openly come out on television in Mexico. After that, she pioneered the Mexican Homosexual Liberation Front and led the first Mexican pride parade. Outside of activism, she was an actress and writer! You can have a career, and single-handedly try to end homophobia too!

environment, whether it's in the form of how you treat others or how you treat yourself. **We all carry burdens that have been passed down by the people who raised us, and it is up to us to recognize and release familial patterns that we choose not to carry any longer.**

We talked a lot about what we felt was right in our cores, versus what we were told. I often think back to when I was a child and had no pressures to be anything but healthy; and honestly, back then I was very similar to the way I am now: masculine in my presence, both physical and in demeanor. I lost that part of me for a bit in an attempt to "fit in." I'm happy I chose to be me and regained

it. **I attribute a lot of my "it gets better" attitude to the freedoms that come with growing up.** I choose to be around people with only love to give, while being mindful of Nate's advice, and making sure I too communicate with love.

"It is OK not to have a relationship with blood relatives or anyone abusive."

Tips for Not Giving a F**K

Confidence check-in! How are you? Confidence for everyone comes in waves. **Sometimes you have a stellar day and on others you feel like you look like a potato.** You're never going to be 100 percent of anything 100 percent of the time! Here are some quick tips to maybe give you a boost when you feel pooped.

#1 **Fake it till you make it!** Don't eye roll like this is terrible advice. This is what I LIVED BY in my late teens. **Sometimes people are going to give you weird looks for not wearing makeup, having dyed leg hair, and wearing your favorite baggy T-shirt, but you know what?** I made it work! Positive affirmations and allowing yourself to live authentically are the soil for confidence to grow in! When I stopped wearing makeup to appear more masculine and feel more like me, I also felt super ugly for some time. Even though I hated wearing makeup, I had been taught in my teen years by societal standards that makeup was the root of beauty. I spent a good month unlearning the way I was taught to view myself and discovering what made me feel attractive and comfortable in my own skin. A portion of that deconstruction was faking it—unapologetically rocking my new look—until I "made it" and I felt better than ever being me.

#2 **Surround yourself with supportive people.** Sometimes this can't apply to everyone, as your folks or family members may not be the most supportive people right now. Do you have a support group of people who see the real you either online or off? Are you holding on to friendships or romantic relationships with people who are constantly putting you down or trying to change you? **Be mindful of who you choose to let into your life and how you both encourage each other to be the best.**

HOW TO SURROUND YOURSELF WITH GOOD PEOPLE

iHop MBET N GREET VIDCON 2017

#1

Sense a vibe. You have a say about who you let in and who's in the inner circle.

#2

Ask yourself who gets the key to your house—think about this both theoretically and literally. Who is that person?

#3

You can always make more friends. Changing who you are for the sake of people liking you will leave friendships feeling unfulfilling and exhausting. You are great! And you should be celebrated, not manipulated.

WHAT DOES IT MEAN TO YOU?

I was freshly out as transgender, plucked from my Los Angeles home, and lost on the streets of Houston, Texas. I was on my first tour and trying to find my way to my hotel with my tour manager after doing a show for local queer kids. My phone was out of range of service, and I'd resorted to aimlessly walking at sundown, hoping any one of my apps would start working.

At least I wasn't alone. My tour manager and I (though he was equally as lost as I was) passed by a bridge arching over a windy road. We heard a voice growl at us from a distance that said (I kid you not), "I am the troll who lives under this bridge. Answer my riddle, and I'll let you pass." So, of course, my dumbass yells back, "What's the riddle? Tell me this riddle." My tour manager starts dragging me away, but we were too slow. This man approaches us wearing a tattered white shawl and brown sandals, and he was reciting beautiful poetry. (Now that I think about it, he easily could've been Jesus.)

He continues to walk with us while reciting his poem. Full theatrics! I'm talking full iambic pentameter for the next ten minutes. Finally, he stops. We're still lost, but now with a new friend. He looks at me and goes, "My riddle is, what does that poem mean?" *Pffft*. Did I look like I took AP English? I laughed and told him I had no idea. He leaned in and told me to listen closely because I need to remember this for the rest of my life. (Definitely Jesus.)

The answer is: It means whatever you want it to mean. He goes, "It doesn't matter what you're doing, and it doesn't matter what anyone has to say about it, what matters is what it means to you." This is the only part of the book where I'm not going to give any input or else that man may literally come and haunt me. Who knows? What does it mean to you?

189

Girls / Girls / Boys—Panic! At The Disco

Lgbt—cupcakKe

Follow Your Arrow—Kacey Musgraves

If You're Over Me—Years & Years

Dance To This—Troye Sivan, Ariana Grande

Girls Like Girls—Hayley Kiyoko

i'm so tired...—Lauv, Troye Sivan

Pussy Is God—King Princess

Boys In The Street—Seeb, Greg Holden

True Trans Soul Rebel—Against Me!

1950—King Princess

Make Me Feel—Janelle Monáe

I Know A Place—MUNA

Mother's Daughter—Miley Cyrus

New Year's Eve—Mal Blum

Told Ya So—Adult Mom

Well, there it is! That is everything you need to know about how to navigate this complicated world! Well, maybe not everything, but some things. My hope for the future is that kids won't have to "come out," but that instead, as they grow and they discover who they love and who they are, it won't be up for debate by someone else. Life isn't about gay versus straight or cis versus trans; it's about everyone feeling content and coexisting in diversity. **I hope you have fun making so many mistakes until you find who you are and who you love.** It's never too late to board a train or call someone back. I went through a lot of adversity and doubt, but I made it out just fine. I hope you will too!

LGBTQ+ FLAGS!

Just like the flow of labels going in and out of use, there have been many symbols used to celebrate sexualities and gender identities over time. Some were designed for pride events like the rainbow flag was in 1978. (Yeah, the rainbow flag has only been around since the late seventies!) Some symbols have been reclaimed, then fallen out of use like the pink-and-black triangles once forced upon gay men and women in concentration camps in Nazi Germany. It was later reclaimed as a symbol of resistance and a community fighting for freedom without persecution.

There are so many flags that have been created to celebrate diverse identities! It may just seem like a jumble of colors, but those colors have been symbols of hope for those who have had to fight to be who they are. Here are just a few flags and who they stand for.

ACTIVITIES:
HOW TO MAKE A VERY GAY CAKE

RAINBOW CAKE RECIPE!

There are so many occasions this cake can be made for:

- To celebrate your recent gay victory. You totally asked that person out so now you totally deserve some cake.
- Be the centerpiece to a coming-out party. Why not have an excuse to throw a party?
- Used to prank an unsuspecting (or unsupportive) family member. Come on, no one can be mad when they get cake!
- A tool in your masterplan to come out. "Hey parental unit, I baked you a cake. It's a gay cake . . . I am similar to this gay cake." You may want to play with the wording but, like I said, come on, no one can be mad when they get cake!

WHAT YOU'LL NEED

- Box cake mix (This isn't a cookbook. I'm just trying to spread some positivity to the young gay kids with the power of tasty treats.)
- Literally, anything the box cake mix tells you you'll need.
- Gel food coloring (it's thicker than liquid food dye, which will result in a more vibrant final product)
- 6 bowls
- 6 baking tins
- Any color frosting

STEPS

1. Mix your cake mix like you would with any standard non-gay cake.
2. Separate the mix equally among your 6 bowls.
3. Fold your food gel and cake mix into each other by color. Red, orange, yellow, green, blue, and purple.
4. Now bake! To save oven space, you can cook 3 tins at a time for 15 minutes each or until she has risen and baked to perfection.

Now you have rainbow cakes you can level, stack, and frost like a normal baking bitch. When someone cuts out a slice, they will be struck with an array of gay!

ACTIVITIES:
HOW TO MAKE
COLORFUL CHALK BLASTERS

Connect with your inner child with this messy and colorful activity! By combining a few ingredients, you will have colorful powder to throw at friends, on yourself, or in the air! Splatter rainbows and take fun pictures of you and your friends coated in rainbow dust—there are no rules! Let go and feel free!

HERE IS WHAT YOU'LL NEED:

- Cornstarch
- Food dye (gel food dye works great!)
- Water
- Gloves (so your hands don't get messy!)
- A big bowl for mixing

INSTRUCTIONS:

1. Preheat the oven to 175 degrees Fahrenheit.
2. Pour 1 cup of cornstarch into a mixing bowl.
3. Add food coloring (your choice on color).
4. Add in ¾ cup of water.
5. Add another cup of cornstarch.
6. With your hands (protected by latex gloves), mix all the ingredients.
7. Pour the mixture onto an oven-safe baking sheet and bake for 1 hour.
8. Check in every 20 minutes to stir the mixture.
9. Remove the mixture from the oven and blend until it is ground into a powder.

Now you have your colorful chalk blaster! Place handfuls into individual baggies so you can grab and throw them with your hands, or wrap handfuls in tissue and throw them like a snowball!

RESOURCES

I used several sources to help research the historical sections mentioned in this book! If you want to know more about any of the queer and trans trailblazers, here are some resources:

- **Biography.com**
- **Bust.com**
- **Glaad.org**
- **Poetryfoundation.org**
- **Stop-homophobia.com**
- **Womenshistory.org**

And the following are resources I trust for additional support, affirmation, and allyship:

- **gsanetwork.org** (get started with a GSA club at school)
- **Trevorspace.org** (a safe space to chat with queer youth online)
- **Bravetrails.org** (LGBT summer camp)
- **Encircletogether.org** (after-school safe space for LGBT Utah youth)
- **Glsen.org** (providing tools for safer schools)
- **Gc2b.co** (trans-owned company that makes binders)
- **Pridecounseling.com** (online LGBT therapist)
- **TrevorText 24/7** (crisis text hotline)
- **Trevor Hotline for suicide prevention** 1-866-488-7386
- **TrevorChat** (instant messaging with a counselor)
- **Thetrevorproject.org**
- **Myfriendsplace.org** (serving LGBTQ+ homeless youth)
- **Pointofpride.org** (making transitioning accessible for all)
- **Transreads.org** (transgender reading material)
- **Gaychurch.org** (LGBTQ+ churches near you)

GLOSSARY

The cool thing about language is that it's continuously evolving to better fit and describe an ever-changing world. If you look at the history of the label you identify with, you may find that it is a relatively new term. If so, then it is up to you to continue to create art, speak up, and educate others on the terms and labels you cling to. Or if you're feeling it, blaze a trail with a new label, or don't ascribe to one at all. You do you! But still, it's always good to know the words in circulation today, so here are some definitions to get you started.

AFAB/AMAB: Assigned Female at Birth/Assigned Male at Birth. I was at the LGBTQ+ medical center when I was referred to on a clipboard as AFAB for the first time. Pretty self-explanatory.

Ally: A person who does not identify as a specific LGBTQ+ label but supports and advocates for LGBTQ+ rights.

Binder: A binder is what AFAB people can use to bind their breast tissue, so it appears more masculine. I wore binders for years, even before I found my transgender identity, as they are not exclusive to the transmasculine community. Safe binders can be purchased from trans-owned websites and businesses.

Bisexual: Attraction to guys and girls; doesn't matter if they are cis or trans since trans men are men and trans women are women.

FTM/MTF: Female to Male Transgender/Male to Female Transgender. These abbreviations are used in the transgender community to define types of transitions.

Gay: Attraction to someone of the same gender.

Gender Dysphoria: This is the feeling of incongruence and disconnectedness from the gender a person was assigned at birth and the gender they identify with. I felt this dysphoria both socially and physically. I talked about gender dysphoria with a gender therapist as I pursued my transition.

Gender Euphoria: The feeling of happiness a person experiences when their gender is correctly identified, and they are recognized as their authentic self.

Gender Expression: The way a person presents themselves on the outside to communicate how they feel on the inside. Everyone's gender expression is different, and it doesn't always mean that men dress traditionally masculine and women dress traditionally feminine. Some boys wear dresses; some nonbinary folk practically live in their hoodies; some girls rock a suit!

Gender Marker: A letter or symbol designating your gender on a form or document. This may include "M," "F," or "X."

Genderfluid: A term for people who do not have a fixed gender. Their gender is in constant movement as if on a sliding scale. Some days they feel more male when other days they might feel more female.

Homophobia: Prejudice against queer people of any kind.

HRT: Hormone Replacement Therapy is used to masculinize or feminize secondary sex characteristics. I started testosterone injections when I was twenty-one as a part of my transition. Not everyone who is trans can or wants to medically transition in this way.

Intersex: People whose bodies aren't strictly male or female by birth. They can be born with many different variations of sex characteristics, whether it be hormones, chromosomes, genitals, or reproductive organs.

Nonbinary/Genderqueer: A term for people whose gender doesn't fit the binary of male and/or female. These people can experience a combination of the two, falling in between or something entirely different!

Pansexual: Attraction to all genders. Many pansexual people define this as being attracted to the person and not seeing gender.

Pronouns: He! She! They! He/him are masculine pronouns. She/her are feminine pronouns. They/them are genderless. I use both he and they.

Queer: That's what I am! An umbrella term that encompasses a multitude of sexualities that doesn't fall under the category of exclusively heterosexual. It was once a derogatory term that has been reclaimed by many young people who find words like "gay" too limiting.

Transgender: That's what I am too! The way this term was first taught to me is that sex is what's between your legs and gender is what's between your ears. Think of transgender sort of like transportation. It isn't defined by the vehicle or the way you move—by car, by boat, by walking, by plane—it's just the movement, from one point to another. In this case, a movement of gender identity, not the steps you take to get there.

Transition: The steps taken to affirm the gender you identify as. A transition can include social, legal, and medical changes. My transition included a social transition where people close to me began calling me by a new name and using alternative pronouns. I also underwent a medical transition. I take male hormones and I underwent top surgery. Legally, I changed my name and gender marker on official documents. Not everyone's transition looks the same. Some people don't have access to or want to undergo specific changes to affirm who they are.

Transphobia: Prejudice against transgender people.

Two-Spirit: An umbrella term for gender-variant indigenous North American people.

Gallery of

FAN

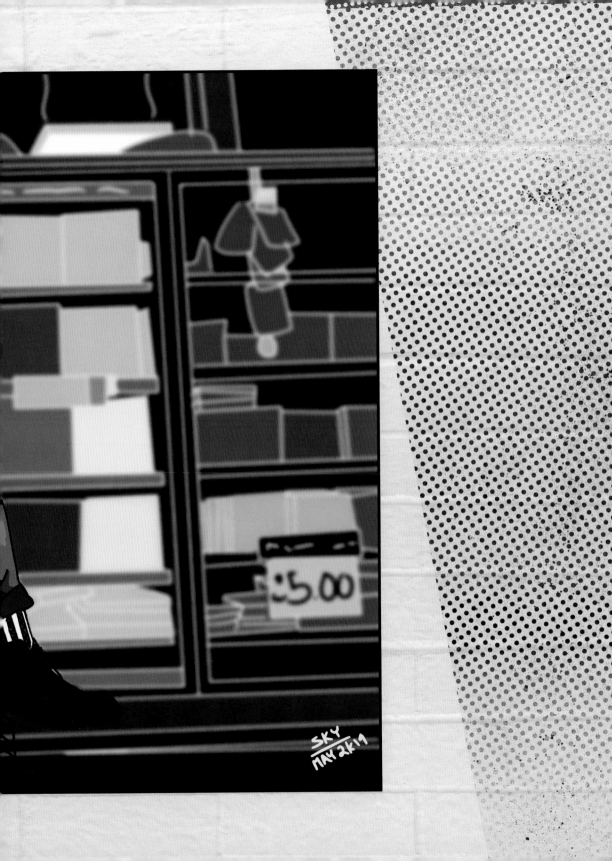

ACKNOWLEDGMENTS

Thank you to Stevie Boebi, a fierce advocate for queer sex education/role model and mentor to me for years. The matriarch to my chosen family. Thank you for letting your home be a safe space for me to run to.

Thank you to my team! Noah Winter and Mahzad Babayan, thank you for being my industry parents and allowing me to be myself. I've learned so much in these few short years from both your honesty and ability to listen.

Thank you to my mother for relentlessly loving your child. And for learning and growing as a parent. "Wherever we go, whatever we do."

Thank you to my love for your endless support, laughter and wit. I am continuously inspired by you, babe. I love you.